Sales SUCCESS *Secrets*

IDEA-RICH SECRET SELLING TIPS

VOLUME ONE

SALES SECRET

Bob 'Idea Man' Hooey
Author, Think Beyond the FIRST Sale

Many thanks...

These two volumes of **Sales Success Secrets** were created with the support of many amazing people in my life. First and foremost, my wife, **Irene Gaudet** who both encourages me and does my editing and formatting.

Thanks to my friends and colleagues: **Peter Chapman, Joanne Blake, Terry Pithers, Barbara Glanz, Joe Bonura, Patricia Fripp, Tim Breithaupt, and Jill Konrath** for kindly allowing us to share your wisdom in Volume One.

My thanks to my amazing friend and former client, **Kim Yost** who was a catalyst to creating the original **Secret Selling Tips** and to Team Brick for all their help back then. We drew on 3 years of bi-weekly issues (2007-2009) in creating these two volumes for you.

My thanks to our readers and audiences around the globe who show up ready to engage and learn together.

Enjoy!

Bob 'Idea Man' Hooey

PS: If you'd like to equip and motivate your sales teams, drop me a note: bhooey@mcsnet.ca Visit www.ideaman.net

Idea-Rich Secret Selling Tips...
How It Came Into Existence.

15-years ago, I had lunch with **Kim Yost,** then CEO of a large Canadian national retail furniture and appliance firm. I had worked with Kim for several years; training their 22 VPs, helping create a book (**The Brick Way**) to enhance and reinforce their culture, coaching their executives in presentations, as well as writing for their internal magazine.

As we came to the finish of our lunch, **Kim** mentioned he needed to find a way to help his 1500 salespeople across Canada become more effective, focused, and profitable. We dialogued some ideas and in less than 15 minutes had outlined the basic idea for what would become our online, bi-weekly **Secret Selling Tips**. I mentioned it sounded like something he could use. He said yes! I asked him how much he thought it would be worth? He mentioned a figure. ☺ I smiled and we launched the English version a month later and the French one shortly after that.

I approached this as one way to serve this leader, who had become a good friend. What I didn't see was this customer service focus would lead to a completely new on-line business for us. He invited me to share what we'd done with 9 of his counterparts south of the border.

I created a small **Pocket Wisdom motivational companion: The Secret Selling Tips** as an incentive to help close my offer and challenged them to sign up their entire sales force. 4 of them signed up their entire teams that day in Chicago, Ill.

Wow! This simple service idea started generating $35-50K a year helping sales professionals across North America. We added short video clips and additional expert articles. We also added single and group subscriptions to serve other smaller organizations. We renamed it **Sales Success Secrets** for this two-book format.

3

Welcome to Sales Success Secrets – Volume 1

We look forward to working with you, to help you equip and motivate yourself to enhance your sales skills and increase your commissions. We are dedicated to your success in the highly competitive sales game.

Each **Sales Success Secrets** chapter has easily applied selling tips, techniques, and tools to help **equip and motivate you in your 'Visionary' quest to be a top performing sales professional. Most** chapters are designed to be read in less than 5-minutes.

Before we start, here is how this works.

- Read a chapter daily with a view to refreshing, adding to, or reinforcing your sales thinking and abilities.
- Each chapter will contain a **'Challenge'** which is great for discussion with your fellow sales team members. We believe in the leveraged power of applied teamwork.
- Each chapter will have an inspirational **'Point to Ponder'** to think about as you go through your day.

'Sales is very much a mental game and keeping focused on your success will help motivate you to succeed.'

We are committed to helping you make that 'BIG' Sales Goal a reality. We are *excited* about the possibilities for you to create amazing success this year (*more later*). We are *excited* about helping you **'visualize'** and **'realize'** your success in the sales game. We are *excited* to be part of your *'virtual'* success team. **Enjoy Volume One.**

Bob 'Idea Man' Hooey
Author, Thinking Beyond the FIRST Sale

Table of contents

Sales Success Secrets

Dedicated to Our Clients, Who May Choose, at Times, To Be Our 'Customers'

As you read, perhaps you will notice that we do not *exclusively* refer to 'customers', choosing instead to employ the descriptive word **'clients'**. This is a deliberate word choice in our vocabulary and a foundational change in mindset necessary to move beyond the FIRST sale into a long-term mutually beneficial relationship with your clients.

Client vs. Customer: Aren't they really the same thing? Webster's defines these two seemingly interchangeable words as:

Customer: one that purchases a commodity or service

Client: one that is **'under the protection'** of another; a person who engages the professional advice or services of another

Ever wondered why the sales superstars sell so much better and make so much more money than their counterparts? One secret is in how they visualize and more effectively approach everyone, which results in such high levels of success. **They see clients vs. customers**, walk into their locations and act accordingly. We hope you will too!

Challenge: Take a moment and reflect on the differences in the meanings of these two words. The way a person, who does business with you, can be approached and treated will directly impact your sales results.

The key to this mental shift lies in understanding what **'under the protection'** of another means in your client interactions.

My thought: this means you don't sell someone a service or product 'just' to ensure you make the largest short-term profit or commission possible. You **serve them best** by helping them *fully* explore their options to make the *'best choice'* when they purchase something!

"Treat your customers like clients and they will remain customers!" **Bob 'Idea Man' Hooey**

7

Sales Success Secrets

Leveraging Your Sales Success Secrets Investment

"Most beginnings are small, and appear trivial and insignificant; but in reality, they are the most important things in life." **James Allen**, *"As A Man Thinketh"*

We originally created this unique, ***sales success system*** to assist those in the field of sales; to encourage and educate you; to help you become more effective in your role, have more fun, and make more money. If you are new to the sales game, they will provide valuable stepping-stones to your success. If you've been doing sales awhile, each chapter will offer reinforcement and perhaps a refresher of the foundations that will keep you focused and successful. **The 'superb' execution of the basics often leads to unparalleled success.**

We want you to succeed in sales! Your investment in time and this book is critical. **Invest wisely and you will see your sales career soar and your earnings even more so.** These tips are gleaned from some of the top sales professionals across time and they work when you do!

However, as simple and successful as they are, they will not work *'unless'* you do.

We designed most of them to be read in 3-5 minutes, with small bite sized pieces to nibble on from time to time between chapters.

- **Want to *succeed* in sales?**
- **Want to make *more* money?**
- **Want to get *more* out of life?**
- **Want to *gain* respect and increased recognition?**
- **Want to *earn* repeat business and get your clients/customers telling your story?**

Whatever your goal, it is important to realize it will be attained only when you strategically and systematically work towards its achievement.

If you want to be successful, you need to consider these points:

- You are what you do daily.
- As they say, *'first you form your habits and then they form you.'* Choose wisely.
- Decide to form positive, constructive, success building habits.
- The *process* is often more important than the event itself.
- Be willing to endure some short-term pain for long-term gain.
- Don't wait for inspiration, do it today!

Point to Ponder: *"Do not be afraid of greatness!"* Shakespeare

Each day, we become what we *'think'* about the most and what we reinforce by our actions. We tend to follow our mental focus!

Invest a few minutes as you read each chapter to reflect and see where what is discussed impacts or fits with what you are *'currently'* doing in your sales process or career. Do an audit of the basics, to see if you haven't been skipping a few or cutting corners because you've been doing it for a while. I find that to be a common challenge. Skipping essential sales steps is often the cause of a sales slump or ineffective results in conversions or closing ratios. Basics make money!

Talk about what you are learning with your co-workers and manager. Ask for help where necessary. Brainstorm ideas on how to *'best'* apply what you are learning. Set strategies in place so each of you reinforce each other in your commitment to become more effective and make more money. Apply the leveraged learning of your team to catapult your sales career.

Work on one area for improvement at a time. Research has proven this is the most effective way of creating and sustaining growth and improvement in any area of study or skill.

Challenge: Go back and re-read previous chapters from time to time. You'll be amazed how much you pick up on the second and third reading. Reinforcement and repetition work, act on them! **Invest in Volume two and apply those lessons as well.**

The Secret of the Seed!

As some of you may know, I moved out into the country northeast of Edmonton some 20 years ago for a more creative and casual lifestyle.

When I was home from my road trips, I would frequently have coffee with my old buddy Steve (my 94-year-old neighbor at the time) and his two *'younger'* farmer friends (Mike, 80 and Peter, 78 respectively). Sadly all 3 have passed away over the years.

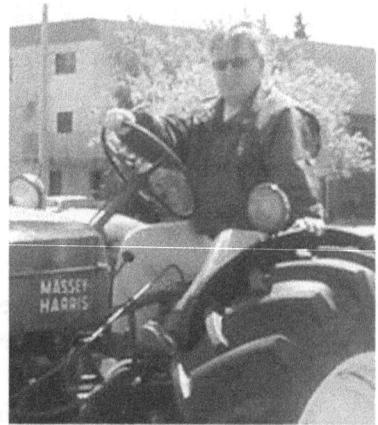

Over those amazing years, I learned a lot about farming that is directly applicable to what we do in life, **sales**, and business.

I've grown to appreciate the effort and challenges our farmers go through to help feed us. They are utterly amazing, hardworking, down to earth, and productive people.

Mike and Peter rotated their crops based on their *'best guess'* at what would be the most profitable for market during the coming year. They planted canola, wheat, barley, oats, or peas, as selected, each year.

When they planted wheat in the spring, they expected to harvest wheat that fall. There was an *'expectation'* that the seeds they planted would produce the crops they planted. They would have been very surprised to plant canola and get barley, for example. **This is the secret of the seed!**

Interestingly enough, I see people planting seeds for failure and then expecting successful or different results in their **sales**, business, or life. They are then surprised when things fail or don't work to their misguided expectations.

Point to Ponder: *Here is the secret of the seed: You get what you plant, nurture, and harvest.*

Plant the seeds *of creative, personal leadership and responsibility;*

Plant the seeds *of continuous encouragement, to dream and stretch;*

Plant the seeds *of equipping your team with the tools and the motivation to win;*

Plant the seeds *of personal discipline and long-term focus;*

Plant the seeds *of co-operative innovation and competition;*

Plant the seeds *of high standards and personal excellence in customer service;*

Plant the seeds *of creating value-added products and superior services we (customers) actually need;*

...and harvest abundance and success at the end of your labours.

Challenge: Pause a moment and revisit your expectations. Give some thought to how you are currently working to make them a reality.

PRO-tip: Think of your sales meetings with customers as a chess game.

You need to be thinking at least 2-3 meetings out. You might want to plant the seed about a new item in development or perhaps an inevitable cost increase. Create content for meetings with customers as a series, not one meeting in isolation. You should always be trying to anticipate what would make the difference down the road. The sales cycle is different from every product, so you need to look beyond and figure out how to wow your customer to get the next order. When I was on the buying-side I looked forward to appointments with suppliers who could help me see the future.

© **Peter Chapman**, *www.gpsbusiness.ca ...with permission*

11

Are You Getting All the Sales You Need? A Foundation Check-Up

Taking time to reflect on your sales performance and follow through is certainly time well invested. Why not reflect on some of these as you go through your day?

- **How are things going recently? Over the year, so far?**
- **Are your sales figures where you expect them to be?**
- **Are you doing well in your conversion and closing ratios?**

If your clients get the impression that you or your staff are indifferent to them or their needs, they will leave. Indifference can creep into even the best sales career or business. That perceived indifference 'will' cost you business and referrals.

Challenge: Are you getting all the sales or business you can?

If not, then a little honest self-inspection might be helpful. A few years back, a fellow sales professional shared some questions with me that I found extremely helpful. Thought I would pass them along, with my thoughts, for your reference and reflection. **You need to track your performance to enhance your performance.**

Take a minute and answer the following questions with a simple yes or no. Mark each yes with a (+) and each no with a (-).

- Do you personally thank your internal customers – your team members and suppliers – for being a productive, integral part of your business success?
- Do you make sure they are well informed about new things happening in your business or affecting your industry?
- Do you ever surprise them or reward them with a small gift or acknowledgement?

- Do you make a point to stay in touch with current clients on a regular basis? (*This is a critical component of sales*)
- Do you normally follow up with clients shortly after they've dealt with you to ensure they are happy with their purchase or service?
- Do you consistently answer the phone on the second ring?
- Does a caller get asked for permission, if you need to put them on hold?
- Do you ensure no one waits on hold for more than 30 seconds without checking to see if they can continue holding or dealing with their call? (*Courtesy works*)
- Do you have an on-hold message for them to listen to?
- Do you thank your clients or potential clients for calling you?
- Do you thank them for buying from you?
- If you are unsuccessful in helping them, do you thank them for the opportunity anyway? (*They might another time.*)
- Do you and your staff arrive on time for any client appointments or meetings? (*This is a critical success trait for sales professionals.*)
- Do you or your team ever make your clients wait?
- Do you consistently deliver products or services when agreed?
- Do you let your clients know ASAP (beforehand) if there is a problem or hold up in the process?
- Do you offer solutions or alternatives if there are any?
- Do you return client calls and messages the same day they are received?
- Does each team member make a commitment to take responsibility for helping clients or do they hand off client problems from department to department? (*Sales secret of the superstars*)
- Do you ask for more information when you're asked about the price of a product or service? (*Draw them out and then answer*)
- Do you make sure you understand what they need your product or service for and that what they select is the best item or service to do the job? (*Pre-qualifying works*)
- Do you thank your clients or potential clients for coming in to visit your business? (*regardless of whether they buy or not*)
- Do you ask satisfied clients who they know who might also be able to use you? (*Referrals are golden!*)

- Do you follow up on those referrals in a timely manner?
- Do you reward clients for referrals who buy from you?
- Do you and your staff meet on a regular basis to brainstorm better ways to serve your clients and for better ways of operating your business?

There is no right or wrong in this check-up. However, reflecting on the results to your questions can give you an indication of areas where you are potentially losing sales or missing opportunities to sell and service your clients more productively and profitably.

Point to Ponder: *Treat each month as a new year and start anew. Your sales goals should be monthly to lead to where you need to be annually.*

Good luck and good selling!

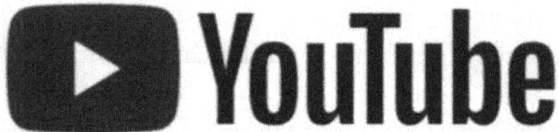

Partway through our 1st SST year, I discovered I could book time in The Brick film studio to record videos for our program. I booked about once a month and we soon added videos to each on-line issue we sent out to our clients across North America.

Recently, we have been converting those sales videos to another format and uploading them to YouTube along with my other videos and recordings from around the globe. Feel free to check them out for yourself. We will keep adding to them. **Please share this link and subscribe to be notified of new videos.**

www.youtube.com/user/ideamanbob

Sales Success Secrets

> "Set a goal so BIG, that if you achieved it, it would blow your mind."
> W. Clement Stone

Thanks for joining Sales Success Secrets family.

Even though we may be past the start of your sales year; remember *'today'* is always a good day to re-visit, re-set your goals, and re-start on their achievement.

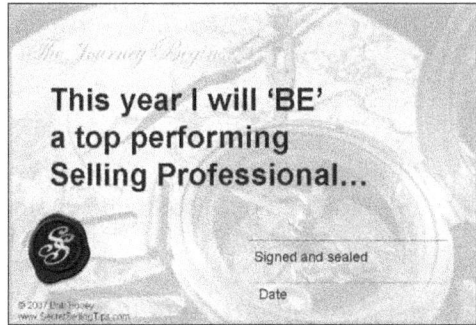

This year I will 'BE' a top performing Selling Professional...

Signed and sealed

Date

HINT: Before you consider setting and writing down that BIG, 'Visionary' sales goal, mentioned in our leading quotation; take a moment to *'imagine'* yourself a year from now. **(Today's date: _____)**

Ask yourself:
- How much *better* are you at qualifying by asking the right questions?
- How much *better* are your conversion and closing ratios?
- How much *better* are your sales volumes?
- How many *additional* repeat customers have you nurtured?
- How much *more* money and commissions have you generated?

Give careful thought to these five *'key'* sales questions. Be as specific as you can in your answers. Dare to *'imagine'* yourself, as you could be, a year from now.

- Can you *imagine* your excitement in looking back and seeing this amazing growth and success in your sales career?
- Can you *imagine* how would that feel?
- Can you *imagine* how your lifestyle would change? How would that *feel?*

This is *your* time! This is *your* career in sales! Your choices and actions, guided by your answers, impact your destiny and success in Sales. How successfully you **visualize** them will dramatically impact how they will unfold for your own success in sales. We believe you have the power within you to succeed.

Now comes the fun part, setting that '*amazing*' goal. Take a few minutes and **"Set a goal so BIG, that if you achieved it, it would blow your mind."** As challenged by **W. Clement Stone**

Remember, this is not a time to play it safe. This is not a time to set a goal you feel you can *easily* reach. This not a sales quota, this is a BIG professional sales goal. Set the goal so BIG, you will push yourself in reaching it. Your goal might even scare you a bit. That is great!

- *Ever thought about being in the million-dollar club?*
- *How about doubling or tripling your commissions?*

My Sales Success Secrets
BIG, 'Visionary' goal for _____:

_____

Visualize it! Write it! Achieve it!

Abraham Lincoln advised, **"*Always bear in mind that your own resolution to success is more important than any other one thing.*"**

REMINDER: Your BIG, '*Visionary*' goal should be much larger than your sales quota if you really *desire* to succeed. Remember the secret behind the idea here is to challenge yourself to stretch and grow, not just reach an *easily* set quota.

Now, that is a goal worthy of your '*best*' efforts!

The secret to profitable sales success is to *keep focused* and *keep moving* forward.

Challenge: Ask your sales colleagues and manager to help keep you focused on achieving *'your'* personal, written BIG, 'Visionary' sales goal.

Just as asking for the order *several* times in the sales process will dramatically increase your chances of gaining the sale; asking for support and encouragement will help you reach your goal in sales this year.

Years ago, when we first launched our on-line sales success program, one of our US clients hired me to come and speak to their 350 sales team members to help them launch it. During my talk I asked them if they wanted to know how to double or triple their sales? Hands flew up across the room. I simply said, **ask for the order at least twice in each sales conversation.** *Most of you are ask resistant and seldom ask even once! One of their senior sales ladies later told me I hit the nail right on the head.* **If we don't ask, we don't get!** *This secret applies to many aspects of life so screw up your courage and ask for what you want. I have used it for great success in several ventures in both business and volunteer roles.*

Point to Ponder: *"The key to success at SONY, and to everything in business, science, and technology for that matter, is never follow the leader." Masaru Ibuka, founder and honorary chairman*

HINT: Throughout generations, those sales professionals who generated the most *consistent* earnings and growth, often asked for help. They were frequently the first to sign up for additional training or to purchase and devour the latest books, programs, and DVDs on sales.

Their sales success secret: They were hungry to learn, to grow, and to succeed! They took personal leadership and responsibility for their own sales careers. Within your own organization there are many who have followed this path to sales success. We encourage each of you to follow their lead. If you bought this book, you are one of them! ☺

Better yet, forge your own path for those who will follow your lead.

"Always aim higher that you believe you can reach. So often, you'll discover that when your talents are set free by your imagination, you can achieve any goal." Edmund O'Neill

Sales Success Secrets

Personal Connections Are Critical

"Getting people to like you is only the other side of liking them."
Norman Vincent Peale

Picture this: Have you ever walked into a retail store and stood there looking, *in vain*, for someone to help you?

Have you seen groups of employees (*I wouldn't call them professional salespeople*) standing together, talking, and tried to catch their attention?

Or watch as one of them *reluctantly* tears themselves away and walks over to ask *'What you want?'* They might even be *'programmed'* to say, *'May I help you?'* Can you picture that in your mind?

Tip # 2:
Make your customers feel *welcome;* but don't pounce on them immediately.

SECRET
SELLING
TIPS

Let's take a different snapshot. Have you ever been in a store and been *pounced on* by an over-eager salesperson who obviously wants to *'sell you'* something? Ever defended yourself with, *"No thanks, just looking!"* even though you had come in with a specific purchase in mind? I have, all too often.

How did you feel in either of these situations?

My guess, not so great, right? What went through your mind at the time? Well, that is what your potential customers have in the back of their minds when they walk into your store, or when you walk into their office or business.

People are a bit nervous when dealing with salespeople... they are **afraid** we are going to **'sell'** them something. Interestingly enough, people love to buy; they just don't like being sold.

In a previous chapter we talked about the importance of setting goals, and we challenged you to *'set one so big, that if you achieved it, it would blow your mind.'*

To make that **BIG, 'Visionary' Sales goal** a reality, you need to interact more *effectively* with your potential customers. Whether you are prospecting, making on-site or virtual sales calls, or working in a retail environment, understanding and applying the *foundations of success in sales* are important. My friends at The Brick (*one of my national clients at the time we created this on-line sales program*) called this their **Seven Steps of Selling** (*used with permission*). I'd like to focus on this one to start.

Sales Step: Confidently greet your clients/customers with enthusiasm

At its most basic level, the opening or greeting is an *initial* step or foundation to establish connection and build trust with a potential client/customer. The windows of attention, where you have the opportunity to build connection, are typically short in duration.

It has been repeatedly proven that **people do *more* business with those they like and trust.**

As a committed **sales professional**, a crucial part of your role is to create that environment where your potential client/customer feels comfortable and open to working with or buying from you. An environment where they feel you are there to help them. (*This can be in a retail setting or when you make a phone, Zoom, or on-site visit.*)

This is not the *qualifying stage* where you find out specifics or probe their needs; it is simply your opening or introducing yourself and your company in *conversational* dialogue. This is the beginning of your sales conversation with them. We'll talk about qualifying later.

Keep your opening objective in mind: Create *immediate* interest for additional discussion and engage or connect with the prospect or customer. That means asking open ended questions that encourage your potential customers to talk.

For example:

'Good morning, my name is Bob... What brings you into our store today?'
Or *'Have you seen our special offers on* _____*?'* (maybe your flyer or website). Much better than *'May or Can I help you?'*

The first two *open-ended* questions might get you an informative answer which can begin a productive dialogue. **May I help you?** might easily get you, 'No, thanks... just looking!' Some sales leaders suggest making personal comments about the weather or *'how was the drive to our store?'* **What works** *'best'* **for you?**

We suggest working on this *'key'* sales skill until you have a *collection of conversational openings* that you are fully comfortable in using. Openings that reflect who you are and not just the same ones your fellow sales members use. Keep in mind, if it is too routine, it will sound routine. Also, customers will hear what your team members use. That can diminish the work you have already done when they recognize a *'canned'* opening. **How do you react to a slick, canned, sales pitch?**

Point to Ponder: ***"Every great business is built on friendship."***
J.C. Penny, *founder of the successful retail chain that still bears his name*

Motivation: Remember your role as a sales professional is to *help* your clients/customers find what they need at a price they can afford. **Make it** *'easy'* **for them to do business with you.**

Whichever you approach you use, make sure you ask from the perspective of someone who is *genuinely* interested in 'them' and smile. Make sure your body language reinforces you are glad to see them.

Never underestimate the power of a *genuine* **smile as a foundation for success in the sales game.** Make them feel welcome and not an interruption in your day, and you are on the path to sales success. If you are working in a retail environment, make sure a *new* customer knows you *'see'* them enter your store. Perhaps, you can make eye contact, wave, and smile. Give them a few seconds to orient themselves and *'settle in'* before you walk over, so they don't feel rushed or pounced on. As a professional, I would always introduce myself to potential clients.

If you do get something like, ***"Just looking, or just getting ideas,"*** don't take it as a rejection, simply a reflection that your customer is not ready to open up to you yet. And sometimes they are just looking. Use this as an opportunity to direct them to an area where you have something that might assist them in their exploration. Perhaps you can say, *"Thanks for coming in. We have some amazing products or services. If I knew what you were considering, I would be happy to direct you to that area."*

You can use this as an opportunity to set up a *'check back'* with them. Suppose they really are just looking. Your response might be something like, *"I'm sure you'll find some fantastic items in our store. We are quite proud of what we offer. May I check back with you to see if you have any questions?"* Perhaps, just say, *"I'll check back with you to see if you have any questions, or I can be of any assistance."* Smile, pause, and walk away.

Make sure they know you are there to help, but not feel pressured with you hovering over their shoulders. This sets the foundation for further dialogue on the road to a successful sale and relationship.

Challenge: What is your personal philosophy on sales? Write it down where you can see it and live it!

PRO-tip: Don't sell the steak – sell the sizzle!

Elmer Wheeler created a highly paid living by creating and testing memorable words that help merchants win sales and influence customers back in the late 30's. E.g.: Wheelerpoint No. 4: **Don't ask if – Ask which!**
Now many of them were brand specific and won't transfer, but there is a lesson to be learned in your field. Once he discovered the sizzle in anything, meaning the tang in cheese, the bubbles in wine, the whiff in coffee, the customer was his, or rather his client's. For many years he made his living teaching them to find and describe the sizzle in their products and services.

My challenge is to look at what you sell with an eye and perhaps an ear for the sizzle. Maybe look at the benefits vs features for inspiration as you create words that entice or seduce prospective clients to check you out and eventually invest in what you offer them. Perhaps buy one of his books (still available on Amazon) and learn from the master.

Asking Great Questions to Qualify Customers

"You've got to ask great questions to qualify your prospects and ask for the order. Otherwise, you're wasting your time." Jeff Mayer

Wisdom and experience, gleaned from generations of top sales leaders, teaches us that when you're able to ask *better* questions, you can do a much *better* job of qualifying and helping your prospects become long-term clients/customers.

The true sales professional who invests the time to *'quickly'* qualify their potential customers is the one who will have the best closing ratios and make more money by working with *more* qualified customers.

> Secret Selling Tip # 3:
>
> *Invest time to 'qualify' potential customers, if you want more sales, referrals, and repeat business.*
>
> SECRET SELLING TIPS
>
> www.SecretSellingTips.com
>
> © 2007 Bob 'Idea Man' Hooey www.SecretSellingTips.com

The true sales professional who, once talking to a qualified customer, digs deeper to discover their real needs and wants will be the sales leader in any organization. Very much like the doctor who asks, *'Where does it hurt?'*

Point to Ponder: *"Spend lots of time talking to customers face to face. You'd be amazed how many companies don't listen to their customers."* Ross Perot

Sales Step: The discovery process or how to qualify a potential client/customer

The secret to becoming a H-U-G-E success in sales (in any industry) is to have a comfortable, proven process to qualify potential customers as a part of the sales process. **A systematic, step-by-step process that you follow day-in and day-out.**

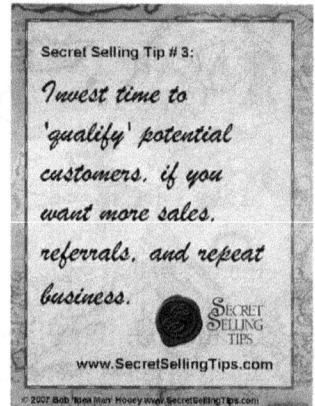

Create and refine your qualifying as part of the sales process and it's easy to increase your revenues and profits without working more hours.

The discovery process is critical in the sales field as a part of pre-qualifying. If you are working in a retail environment, more so one where advertising drives the sales process, a quick way to pre-qualify will save you time and make you more money. Isn't that a better use of your sales time?

For example, a couple visiting a furniture or appliance store to purchase a new fridge. *Our 1ˢᵗ sales success client was a national furniture and appliance retailer, so we started from there as we evolved this sales success program.*

Some questions you might ask them in a retail location:

Questions that draw out what the customer is considering and what features, benefits, and price point would influence their decision to buy. Ask about old appliances as well as a new purchase. For example:

- 'What are the 3 things you would like in a new _____?'
- 'What were the 3 things you didn't like about your old ____?'
- 'What features did you have in mind for your new _____?'

Questions that help narrow the focus to specific choices. For example:

- 'What color scheme did you have in mind?'
- 'Does this piece have a specific color or pattern you like?'

Questions that lead to writing up an order. For example:

- 'When would you like to have that delivered?'
- 'Would you like to have us install it?'

Quick note: If your prospect's answers don't quite measure up to what you think they should be, or don't tell you what you need – and you've made sure you've asked good questions – then in reality, you don't have a good prospect. Or, at least not at the present time.

On the other hand, when the questions do measure up and you've discovered a problem you can solve, you've created a good sales opportunity for yourself.

Think about the previous questions as they apply to your product or service. How can you be prepared to ask the right questions?

Remember to summarize what you've learned in this discovery process before you move to the next action step in solving their problem or showing them something that fits their expressed needs. Inevitably in any conversation things will slip through the cracks or misunderstandings will occur. This is your chance to allow the customer to correct them before you move into either creating a proposal, demonstration, or showing them samples for consideration.

Asking something like:

- *'Is that a fair summary of our discussions?'*
- *'Let me see if I have this correct? What you are looking for is_____.'*
- *'Am I correct in my understanding?'*

Challenge: What questions should you be asking to better qualify your prospects?

Create a list of 10 questions you can use in your specific situation that will draw out the information you need to qualify and then help your prospect.

Refine these questions, revamp them, revise them, replace them until you have some that are thoughtful, insightful, and emotionally engaging questions. Discuss these with your fellow sales professionals. Asking questions your competition doesn't ask is a great way to not only differentiate yourself but reinforce your customer's confidence in your abilities and expertise to take care of them. I did that when I was designing and selling kitchen and bath cabinets and installations.

***"To understand others, you should get behind their eyes and walk down their spines."* Rod McKuen**

Sales Success Secrets

What Makes 'YOU-nique?'

Point to Ponder: *"To my customer, I may not have the answer, but I'll find it. I may not have the time, but I'll make it. I may not be the biggest, but I'll be the most committed to your success!"* **Anonymous**

In a world of increasing 'me-too's' and 'sorta-like's' and 'ditto's' - what makes you stand out from the crowd? What **'YOU-niqueness'** do you bring to the marketplace that will make your potential customers want to deal with you and return time and time again? Are there things you do that your customers aren't expecting? Surprises?

Challenge: Take a few minutes and give some creative thought to these questions. Analyze your answers, for in them are revealed the secrets of your eventual success and competitive edge.

- What do I provide my clients/customers that **they can't get everywhere else**?
- What can I do to follow-up as a thank you to people – even those who don't buy from me now?
- What can I say or give to my customers that will influence them to remember me and the experience they enjoyed with my firm?
- What 'extra-unexpected-value' can I provide my customers after they buy from me?
- What can I give my clients/customers that will totally amaze them – something they would never expect?
- How can I build long term relationships and communicate with clients/customers and their families that will influence them to remember me for years to come?

Based on careful thought – what changes will you commit yourself to making which will ensure these **'You-nique' factors** become part of your daily operation? When will you start? **Start today!**

Sales Success Secrets

Exploring Solutions to Show and Sell

"Advice is like snow; the softer it falls, the longer it dwells upon, and the deeper it sinks into the mind." **Samuel Taylor Coleridge**

Ander and Stern who wrote **'Winning At Retail'** defined service from a client or customer's perspective: (1) knowing what I want and having it in stock; (2) helping me find the product I'm looking for easily without wasting my time; (3) providing information to answer my questions and assist me in making an intelligent choice - with signs, brochures, a salesperson, via the internet; and, after you've done the first three right, (4) having friendly, knowledgeable people. *(Keys to winning the sales game)*

"Explore solutions based on 'qualified' customer needs to move the selling process ahead."

Secret Selling Tips

Sales Step: Exploring or presenting sales solutions

The secret to increasing your conversion and closing ratios is simple: See the process through the eyes of your client/customer. Help them make the right 'buying' decision.

This step will challenge you to do your homework. You need to become and remain a *knowledgeable* expert on your product and services to fully advise and assist your customer in making the right 'buying' decision. Remember, your customer may have done their homework on the web before they came in to see you. They will know when you are bluffing and your credibility as well as your sales will suffer.

In fact, knowing your products and services will help you ask more intelligent, differentiating questions in the qualifying stage of the sales process.

Point to Ponder: *"Purpose is the engine, the power that drives and directs our lives."* John Noe

We wanted to give you a *quick* overview of this critical step in the sales process. Sales professionals make a sale when they show or demonstrate the value of and personalize or translate those features to their customers. The top performers are often the most knowledgeable as well. If you have qualified well, you will already know which features to focus on and can move ahead to demonstrate their benefits and advantages to your customer.

Key to Remember: It is not the features that sell your product or service – it is those benefits or advantages those features bring to your customers. Thinking about and sharing from the benefit/advantage point of your customer is the secret to your long-term success in Sales. It is also the secret to gaining referrals and repeat business.

Simple Sales formula: create a series of **'so that'** advantage statements to help your customer.

This [**Product/Service**] has [**feature**] which means [**benefit**] so that you [**advantage**]. (This leads to creating the solution to a challenge.)

Once you've gone through the qualifying process with your potential customer you can confidently move into the **Show and Sell** (exploring solutions) stage in helping them select the right product or service for their specific needs.

Here are some suggestions to help you successfully navigate this stage in the Sales process. Based on one of the Brick superstore retail locations.

Don't overwhelm them with choices or options. For example: if they are shopping for a TV don't show them the TV Wall. (literally a wall of TVs) Take them directly to the appropriate department or display area.

One secret gleaned from top sales professionals is to give them a choice of 3 and show them the higher/best quality or higher priced selection first. Why, you ask? People like to be in control of their choices and not overwhelmed.

27

Giving them a choice of 3 narrows it down and allows them to 'choose' or buy. Another factor: People will surprise you and might actually buy the higher quality or priced choices. (good, better, best)

'Demonstrate' entails involving them and the rest of their 'buying' party (who can have a direct influence on the decision). Get them to play with the buttons, open the drawers, change the channels in the home theatre room, lie down on a mattress, or sit on the sofa or recliner. Get them involved, let them touch it and enjoy it. Let them experience, if only for a moment, how it would feel to own and use that specific product. This is a great way to differentiate the various features between your three choices which also help in the final decision.

Hint: Be ready to express and demonstrate those features, benefits, and advantages that most meet their expressed and un-expressed needs.

However, be careful in over-sharing your opinion. Your role as the '*knowledgeable*' advisor is that of a resource guide in helping them make the right 'buying' decision, for them.

This is a great opportunity to plant the seeds for an expanded sale. As you learn more about your customer you can *logically* introduce additional components into the mix. For example: accessories, additional pieces (e.g., TV Stand/wall mount), special packages or pricing (e.g., Sofa, loveseat or chair) which will complement their main purchase, fabric protection, payment plans, protection or warrantee programs.

Challenge: How well do you know and describe the features, benefits and advantages of your products and services?

- Invest time to break down and determine the more customer important features for your products and services.
- Make sure you know what benefits (to customer) each of those provide.
- Follow through to determine the advantage (to customer) for each benefit.

Preparing to meet the needs of your customers is an important part of the secret to success in sales and business.

Sales Success Secrets

Objections or 'I'm not sold yet'

"What is the difference between an obstacle and an opportunity? Our attitude toward it. Every opportunity has a difficulty and every difficulty an opportunity." J. Sidlow Baxter

Dealing with objections or concerns is a *valid* part of the sales process. If you've been in sales for a while, you probably consider them normal. Perhaps you've learned how to *minimize* them in advance by being more effective in qualifying customers before moving on to the **Show and Sell** process or into asking for the order.

> "Obstacles (objections) are simply chances to prove you are a professional in helping clients make the right purchase."

This part of the process can come up at any time during the sales process so being aware and being prepared will help you win the day and gain the sale.

For the sales professional dealing with objections, concerns, or stalls is simply a natural part of the sales game. Being unprepared or surprised when a customer brings one up should not happen to the sales professional who has done their job in qualifying.

Understand the difference between a stall and an objection.

Stall: 'I want to think about it!'
Objection: 'Your price is too high.'

Both are put off's and essentially reveal they haven't bought in yet.
- Maybe they perceive too high a risk.
- Maybe they think they can get it cheaper somewhere else.
- Maybe they don't have enough confidence in you to go ahead with the purchase.
- Maybe they aren't the real decision maker.

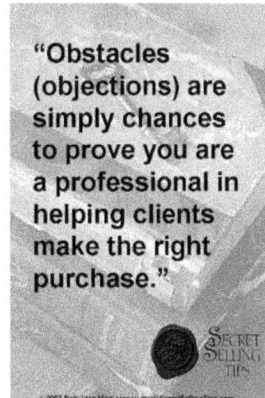

In either case they are giving you the opportunity to help them feel comfortable in making the decision and going ahead with the purchase.

Make sure they are giving you the real reason and not simply putting up a false objection or concern. Many salespeople have spun their wheels trying to answer or overcome false challenges only to be given another and another. Get to the real objection and answer it.

We will delve into this deeper in another chapter. There are several basic objections that can come up:

- **Objection around one of the 4 P's (primarily price)**: Being educated about your company's strengths (P's) as well as your competition is important.
- **Objection around the brand itself:** If a customer is brand loyal or dislikes a particular brand ensure the customer understands the excellent value of the brands you carry. Be willing to present another brand if needed.
- **Objection based on a delay:** Find out who or what is the cause of the delay and work to resolve it on-site, or asap. This goes back to the qualification process.
- **Objection based on knowledge or hearsay:** Occasionally you will find a customer who has '*heard*' something about a particular brand or product. This is where doing your homework in gaining product knowledge comes into play. When you really *know* the product, it is easier to dispel myths or misinformation and support the great value of those products you carry.

Point to Ponder: *"Sales is a series of conversations leading to a series of yeses."*

When I was helping train The Brick teams, we often discussed a 4-step process for handling objections. I share them with you for your consideration.

1. **Empathize with the customer:** Use of the 'feel, felt, found' process. E.g., *"I understand how you feel, many of our customers felt that way until they tried this _____ and they found that..."*

2. **Find the real reason:** Make sure you ask enough questions to ensure this is the real reason. Use this as a chance to re-qualify them and gain addition information to be able to help them further in making the right decision.

3. **Isolate the objection:** Ask if that particular reason was solved, would they be satisfied. For example: *'If we could have this TV delivered to you before Saturday in time for your party would you be interested?'*

4. **Answer or overcome the objection:** Secrets gleaned from top sales professionals teaches the most effective method is to remain focused on the feature, benefit, advantage statements. If you have done your job in qualifying them these should be speaking to their motivation (or hot buttons.)

Don't be afraid of objections. These barriers are an indication that customers want to buy, they just may not want to buy from you yet. As sales professionals our job is to engage them, qualify them, and then help them make a right decision.

Challenge: What are the most common objections or concerns expressed by your customers?

Take a few minutes to think back over your sales career.

- What are the most common concerns or objections you hear?
- How do you handle them?
- Do you have something in mind so that you are not surprised when you hear one? Make sure what you respond with does not sound canned, simply an honest answer in a conversational mode.

Remember sales is really a series of conversations leading to a series of yeses.

"You don't need a big close, as many sales reps believe. You risk losing your customer when you save all the good stuff for the end. Keep the customer actively involved throughout your presentation, and watch your results improve." **Harvey Mackay**

You Have to 'Ask for the Sale'

"Behold the turtle. He makes progress only when he sticks his neck out." **James B. Conant**

Many salespeople are *'ask reluctant.'* Perhaps you find yourself playing this role. It can be overcome!

Remember, the worst that can happen is your customer says 'NO', which to the sales professional simply means, 'Not Yet!'

I believe you owe it to the client/customer to give them a chance to say, 'yes' or 'no'. After all, they came down to see you, didn't they?

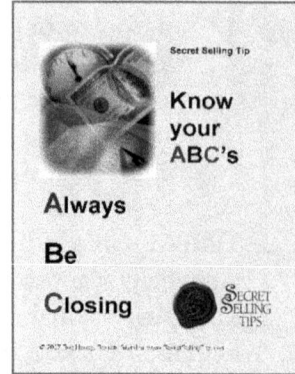

As mentioned earlier, investing time *pre-qualifying* your client/customer, and then helping them based on that information increases the chances of you successfully gaining the sale. If you don't ask, you don't sell. As **Wayne Gretzky** is reputed to have said, *"You're going to miss 100% of the shots you didn't take."* Or, as my sales friends remind me, *"Ask for the sale at least three times, if you want to increase your sales."* **Good advice!**

Sales Step: – Ask for the sale

Recognizing the buying signals. To the astute sales professional, buying signals are the opening to a trial close. Listen to what your client or customer says, (*e.g., Are these in stock? Can we get it by next week?*) and watch what they do (*e.g., couple nods to each other or really gets into the demo*).

HINT: When you ask for the sale – stop selling. **Keep silent and let the customer respond first.** Too many salespeople, me included, have talked themselves out of the sale when the customer wanted to buy. If the client/customer says no or raises an objection, simply move back to qualifying and re-presenting the benefits and advantages.

If you are going for a total plan close (bundling the room) always make sure to close on the main item first. Then, as their '*knowledgeable*' advisor, suggest items you know will compliment, complete, and help them enjoy their purchase. Plant the seed for follow up contact to add to their purchase. We'll go into that when we cover add-ons.

Q: So, when should I close?
A: Every chance you can! (Quick answer)

There will be multiple opportunities to '*ask for the sale*' or '*go for the close*' during the sales process. As a rule of thumb, any time your customer asks a question could be considered a closing opportunity.

The top performing sales professional adds proven tools and techniques to their '*sales toolbox*' which allows them to build relationships and build value en-route to the sale.

Understanding and developing a series of '*conversational*' closes is their secret to sales success. By conversational, we mean natural sounding dialogue with your customer that moves them to the purchase. Your close should be a natural transition and not '*sound*' like a rehearsed, slick pitch, which is the kiss of death in today's sales field.

Point to Ponder: *"The only successful sale is the one that winds up with a satisfied customer."* John F. Lawhon

Throughout Sales Success Secrets we touch on the question of asking for the sale and deal with closing. **Here are 5 of the more common closes in practice.** You may already be using some of them or a variation based on one of them.

Remember, **the only really '*bad*' close is the one not asked.** Far too many customers leave your store to purchase from your competitors. Why would I say that? Because that is *sadly* true in every industry, and I have done it to myself as well.

The Direct Close – simply ask for the sale with a direct closed question. 'Can we get this written up today?'

The Either/Or Close – asks customer for a choice between two products or selections.

The Summary Close – simply summarizes all the good points (Benefits and Advantages) discussed and asks for the sale.

The Turnover or Pass-off Close – keeps the door open for more discussion by inviting a manager or a senior sales rep into the conversation. This is a great technique to help save the sale as well as providing an opportunity to learn. Car dealers do this quite often.

The Urgency Close – Used primarily with *'as is'*, *'floor model sell off'*, *'last in stock'* or in conjunction with special sales and promotions.

Personal note: Professional sales is a *'series of conversations'* focusing on creating a *'series of yeses.'* Asking for the sale is *simply* another conversation to enjoy with your customer. Don't shy away from honoring their commitment of time by **not** asking them to buy from you.

When you have qualified well and have gone through your presentation focusing on those benefits and advantages that appeal to your customer, the close will often be a natural transition in your conversation to completing this part of the sales process.

Challenge: Take a moment to reflect on your sales process over your career.

- How often do you ask for the sale?
- How often have you missed the opportunity and allowed a client or customer to *'think it over'* or use some other excuse to not buy?
- What closing techniques have been the *most* effective for you?

"I think there is something more important than believing: Action! The world is full of dreamers, there aren't enough who will move ahead and begin to take concrete steps to actualize their vision." **W. Clement Stone**

Principles on Power Negotiating Techniques

In the negotiation process, *as a vital part of* the sale process, it is imperative to understand the basic principles that make top-level sales professionals successful. We negotiate everyday with our family and friends, our co-workers to cover for us, with our employers for salaries and perks, and with our clients for sales.

Keeping a few basic principles in mind will allow you to negotiate fairly and increase the chance of getting a double win resolution. This will bring about a better quality of life, and a more profitable and *'sustainable'* sales career.

Challenge: The following points will assist you in becoming a powerful negotiator and being better equipped in the sales process.

- It is better to focus on **how you both can win,** especially if you are client-oriented sales pro that plans on being here for the long-term.
- Regardless of what you want **the other person must be satisfied** or at least feel satisfied with what they got from the result.
- **Separate the people from the problem** or obstacle to reaching a mutually satisfying conclusion. Focus on solving problems and not on emotions wrapped around the problem. Don't make it personal.
- **KNOWING the negotiation style** of the person you are negotiating with is critical to leaving with a positive outcome for both parties.
- **Focus on interests**, and not your positions. Positions can be fixed Each of you may have interests, which need to be met. Fixed items can put your negotiations into a corner.
- **Keep your emotions in check.** Never fall in love with something or you may lose some of your chips in the game. Don't over-react or get mad either! It's not about winning but getting to a mutual win.
- **Listen and question the person you are negotiating with,** as you may discover a better deal than you ever thought was possible.

These principles when properly applied, will give you an increased chance to successfully conclude your negotiation and walk away with an agreement **(SALE)** that will satisfy both parties. If you are committed to gaining repeat business, **this has to be the focus and the foundation of your sales and follow up relationship.**

These success principles apply in both personal and professional situations requiring negotiation. They can assist you in having more satisfying relationships and a more profitable sales career path. Apply them wisely!

Point to Ponder: *"During a negotiation, it would be wise not to take anything personally. If you leave personalities out of it, you will be able to see opportunities more objectively."* Brian Koslow

PRO-tip: But Sir, it's my duty to show you!

About 13 years back, I visited an authentic Indian gift shop (5 floors) while speaking in Mumbai, India. After touring the store, we were brought into a seating area and served tea. A nice man started bringing out trays of jewellery: pearls, diamonds, emeralds, etc. He asked if I liked them and then proceeded to bring out more trays. Wow!

I made the attempt to let him know I wasn't going to buy any jewelry as I had already bought a lovely scarf for my wife. His response was to shrug his shoulders, smile, and say, **"But sir, it is my duty to show you!"** Twice! Then, I made the mistake of asking if he had any garnets. Why not look, I thought? ☺

PS: My wife loved the box cut garnet earrings and matching garnet necklace I gave her for her birthday the next week when we met in Paris on my way home. Service works as a sales tool!

© **Bob 'Idea Man' Hooey,** *Excerpted from 'Make ME Feel Special!'*

Do You Ask the Million-Dollar Question?

Perhaps you are already in the *'million-dollar'* **sales club.**

Congratulations! But if you aren't, learning to ask the million-dollar question will propel you in that *'profitable'* direction.

If you are dedicated to being a top-level sale *'professional'* and giving each client your best service and expertise, failing to ask for 'it' undermines all your hard work to date. After you've qualified them and shown them items that take care of their needs, then what? What do you do to help them make a more informed purchase?

Ask each customer to consider additional items to make their purchase better *"for them"*

This is where your experience and expertise come into play, as well as your powers of observation and honed active listening skills.

Secret Selling Tips

© 2007 Bob Hooey, Guardian of The Secret Tips www.SecretSellingTips.com

During your time leading up to the close or order, you've been watching and listening to your clients and have a better idea of what they like, don't you? You've already seen some opportunities to help them enhance their enjoyment with the item or items they intend to purchase.

Sales Step: Add-on items or services as a part of the order

The secret to becoming a *'million-dollar'* sales professional is simple: Ask qualified clients to purchase additional pieces, services, plans, or complimentary items to make their purchase more enjoyable or work better. Sell them what they need to get the most from their purchase. That is where you prove you are a true professional. This commitment will make your sales numbers and commissions skyrocket.

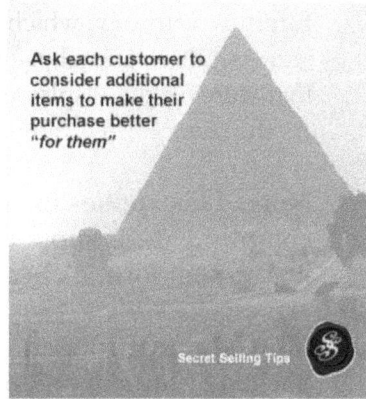

Consider two simple questions from leading fast-food chains: 1) *'Would you like fries with that?'*, or 2) *'Would you like to biggie size or super-size that?'* Training their order takers to ask these simple questions has added **billions, not millions**, to their gross revenues.

A few retail examples: You are selling a TV or sound system… do you think it might be a good idea to suggest a stand that is designed to support, compliment, and augment that TV? Or a wall bracket if it is a flat screen? Or extended warrantees, hmmm!

How about selling a sofa or love seat? Would it make sense to suggest a furniture warranty, which can benefit them? Or how about suggesting or showing them a total package? Or at least suggesting the two pillows that were on the display unit as an accessory? I'm sure you get the idea. As the *'knowledgeable'* advisor you are simply doing your job.

Note: This applies in any industry: is there an add-on that compliments or supports the product or service to make it a better investment for the client?

More about introducing extended protection plans as part of the package. Introduce it earlier in the sales process, so it doesn't appear tacked on. For example: *'Including the extended protection plan this TV is only $895.'* Simple and easy; wouldn't it make sense to mention it?

If consistently asked, these simple, strategic, systematic actions would add-on millions of dollars to your sales.

Point to Ponder: *"Success has a price tag on it, and the tag reads courage, determination, risk taking, perseverance, and consistency – doing the RIGHT THINGS for the RIGHT REASONS and not just when we feel like it."* **James M. Meston**

A few additional thoughts on Add-ons:

- It is easier to add on to a sale with a customer you've been building trust and rapport with than looking for a new one… and more profitable as well.

- If you are smart (not slick) in your presentations suggesting add-ons will be perceived as a sincere effort on your part to help your clients get what they want and need.
- Add-ons should be *primed*, where applicable, along the sales process. They work *'best'* when not just *'added-on'* or hurriedly tacked on at the end. This can be *simply* done as you ask questions in the qualifying stage, during the presentation stage, and even while handling objections. E.g., This is part of exploring the expanded sale and a valid part of bundling a room as a path to selling a larger package.
- In fact, when you suggest or use add-ons *throughout* the sales process to enhance the *'Package tags'* and to reinforce or build perceived value, you will often reduce the number of objections.
- Remember, the worse they can say is 'no'. Often, they will say 'yes'!

Remember: Asking for the order gets you the sale. Asking for additional items along with the order will make you a *'million-dollar'* sales superstar and coincidently a lot more in commissions. Hmmmm!

Challenge: How many opportunities do you have each day to prime the pump and introduce add-ons in your conversations with customers?

- Invest a few minutes to reflect on what kinds of add-ons you can suggest based on what services and products you offer in your store.
- Think too, about where you can *'prime the pump'* and introduce them *'conversationally'* during the sales process.
- Work on them until they are anchored in your mind and become a *'natural'* part of your conversation with each customer.

HINT: You'll notice *'conversationally'* used here again. When you share information in a *'conversational'* manner it is not often perceived as *'selling,'* *'pitching'*, or *'pressuring'* a client. It is, simply *'information'* for their consideration.

This is one of the secrets of the *'million-dollar'* sales superstars.

Are You Building Future Success and Business?

In an earlier chapter, we asked if you were a part of the **million-dollar sales club.** Here are a few more tips to help propel you in that direction and/or help keep you *profitably* anchored at the level.

You've successfully navigated the sales process from first impressions (greeting) moved through the discovery (qualifying) stage, done a great job in sharing features, benefits, and advantages and handled any objections that came up.

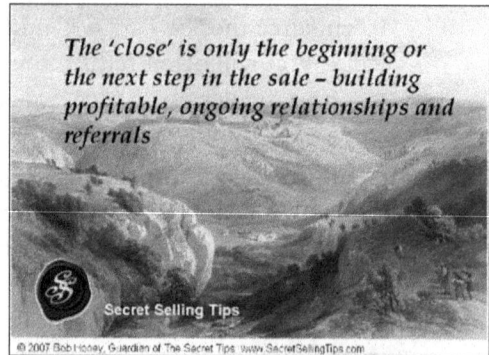

The 'close' is only the beginning or the next step in the sale – building profitable, ongoing relationships and referrals

Secret Selling Tips

© 2007 Bob Hooey, Guardian of The Secret Tips www.SecretSellingTips.com

You've asked for the sale, gotten a yes and even added a few items to help your client, now what? **What would the '*million-dollar*' sales superstars do now?**

Sales Step: Reinforce good decisions and future service.

Another secret of leading sales professionals is based on considering the total lifetime value of your customer. Retail customers can, if serviced well, become long time customers, and create repeat business as well as become a great source for referrals. That part of the sales process begins here, at the close of the initial purchase.

What has to happen before the client/customer gets to enjoy the purchase they made from you?

- Does it need to be ordered, built, delivered, set up, or serviced?
- What is involved in that process that your customer needs to know now?

Taking a minute or two to go over their purchase and what needs to happen is a good investment of their time… it is imperative from your perspective. Doing this reduces the chance they will get home and go through what we call, 'buyer's remorse.' We all go through it at times.

Your role as the 'knowledgeable' advisor is to guide them in this process and to support their decision. That can be as simple as your honest observation, *"John, Pat… You've made a wise investment in this setting or this TV. I'm sure you'll enjoy it for years to come. Thank you for shopping with us, we really appreciate your business."*

Point to Ponder*: "Desire is the key to motivation, but it's the determination and commitment to an unrelenting pursuit of your goal – a commitment to excellence – that will enable you to attain the success you seek."* Mario Andretti

A simple thank you can work wonders in reinforcing your relationship and the good decision they made to deal with you. This is very much a personal decision, and you are part of the consideration too. Your last 60 seconds with your client can be the most important investment in your long term, mutually profitable, relationship. Invest them well.

Remember: **Customers for life is a worthy goal for a sales professional.** *For example, my sister and her husband have bought quite a few vehicles from the same Ford salesman over the years because he takes care of them.*

A few more PRO-tips:

- When you **say thank you**, look your customers in the eyes and '*smile.*' People are so seldom *honestly* thanked; it will help drive home that you are grateful for their trust and business. And you should be. After all, their purchase pays your bills and allows you to take care of your family or enjoy your life, doesn't it?
- **Offer your ongoing assistance.** Make sure they don't leave without at least two of your business cards. Remind them you'd appreciate them passing along your name to any of their friends or family who might also be in the market for _____. Word of mouth is a powerful marketing tool, if you prime them to use it.

- **Remind them of your store/company's commitment** to them and your guarantees. Ask them to call *'you'* if they have any questions. Don't use the word, *'problems'* or say, *'If something goes wrong,'* as that could prime the pump for returns. Be proud, positive, and supportive of what you sell.

- If you have worked up a *total package* for them and they did not buy the whole deal, remind them you will **keep their information on file** for their future use. Let them know you'll let them know about special sales and events coming up. That primes the pump for a follow up call from you or an invitation to come in again. It also allows them to re-consider and add on later.

- **Make sure you keep in touch.** One opportunity might be a quick call to see how they like their new '_____', after it is delivered or set up. *I did that when I was in the design business. I would schedule an installer visit about a month after we were done to come in and make any adjustments needed to make sure everything was great.*

- **Walk them to the door and offer your hand.** This is a great time to personally say thanks again for coming in.

- **Help them to their vehicle if they take purchase with them.** Go the extra mile.

- **Invite them to drop back in** and tell you how their purchase is working out… tell them, *'I'd love to hear from you'*. Again, use your electronic customer file to keep in touch and keep them informed of events and sales that would benefit them.

- **Give them a small gift** or perhaps a coupon for a coffee or Danish on you at a local coffee shop. (*More so if they have just made a substantial purchase.*) Perhaps you can make arrangements with one close to your store to do so.

- Since you have their name and address, why not take *'one'* minute to **pen a handwritten thank you note** (not a form or routine) and drop it in the mail on your way home. Drop another business card inside it too.

Later, we'll tell you the true story of **Johnny the Bagger**… it is an amazing example of what one person can do to show appreciation, and the powerful reaction it can cause. The results of his *'simple'* efforts have allowed the store he works for to gain international recognition as well as increased success and business.

Challenge: How can you reinforce good decisions and set the foundation for future service? This might be a good topic of conversation with your fellow sales team members.

- Perhaps when you are having a coffee or on that '*rare*' occasion when you are standing talking to each other at the back of the store.
- Come up with *specific* ways you can demonstrate or reinforce that your customer made a good decision.
- Come up with *specific* ways to generate future service and additional business or referrals.

Manager's Bonus tip: Mistakes Made by New Sales Staff

Why are senior sales staff more effective and productive in their sales efforts? Could it be that they've learned these simple points that help them sell better?

Lack of preparation. There is an old saying: 'Success happens when opportunity meets preparedness,'

Not listening. 90% of salespeople never listen and are doomed to ineffectiveness.

Failing to ask for the order. Most of the studies I've read show that 70% of all sales folks NEVER ask for the order. Do you, do yours?

Poor or no follow up. Follow up and follow through is where 90% of all great sales are made.

Small thinking. Want bigger sales? You must think bigger. Ask these questions: 'How high is high? What is my maximum potential?'

Failing to establish and/or maintain rapport.

Failing to commit and establish themselves as experts in their field.

Give your team a chance to win by reminding them of these sales' success secret tactics. Remind them to keep focused and keep working toward their goals of helping the client make a decision that is good for the client and profitable for the company.

Dress for Success in the Retail Sales Field

Mark Twain said it best: *"Clothes make the man (or woman). Naked people have little or no influence in society."*

How you present yourself can have a marked impact on your earning power and sales conversions. Just as your company invests time and money designing, building, and detailing your retail environment, sales professionals need to invest in their professional appearance and business attire in order to facilitate a better, more credible connection with their customers. **Dress for sales success!**

Overall, **people like dealing with professionals** and how you dress speaks loudly to that commitment. Dress *sloppily* and they wonder if you will take care of them with that same *lack of attention* to detail. Dress *well* and you underscore your commitment to making their shopping experience a pleasant and mutually profitable one. Dressing appropriately is an investment in your future success. Don't allow how you dress to *detract* or *distract* from your ability to connect, interact, and help your customers *confidently* purchase from you. ***Dress for sales success!***

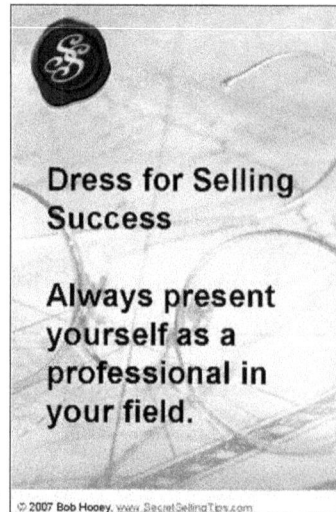

Dress for Selling Success

Always present yourself as a professional in your field.

© 2007 Bob Hooey, www.SecretSellingTips.com

In this chapter we draw on the expertise of one of my friends, **Joanne Blake**, who is an expert (*one of 200 Certified Image Professionals in the world*) in this area. ***"If you look good, you feel good. When you feel good, you sell better!"***

Dressing for Credibility

Business attire is not fashion for fashion's sake and thank goodness it doesn't change every season, but it does follow certain trends and rules. Business attire as part of our personal image is an incredible business tool that is often taken for granted. As competition in our careers, products, and services becomes tougher and more sophisticated, one needs to consider image as an important tool to communicate success.

Rule number one is that business clothing must be business driven. It must promote our credibility and meet client expectations. For the past decade or so this rule has been ignored.

The jacket adds right touch

While the high-contrast suited look (white shirt with dark suit) may be appropriate to some industries (financial/law/insurance professions), many clients respond to a more approachable look. The jacket adds just the right touch in that it is formal enough for most business functions, yet it can be teamed with other wardrobe pieces to give us many different looks. The jacket is an extremely versatile piece of clothing.

The formality of a jacket can easily be softened to convey our own personal style. Men can achieve this by teaming the jacket with a coloured shirt (with or without tie) or a solid-coloured polo shirt or a fine gauge sweater. Women can add almost any top to the jacket as long as not too much skin is revealed (the more skin the less credibility). We put the jacket on to dress up our look or take it off to be more informal.

Point to Ponder: *"An individual's self-concept is the core of their personality. It affects every aspect of human behavior: the ability to learn, the capacity to grow and change, the choice of friends, mates, and careers. It is no exaggeration to say that a strong positive self-image is the best possible preparation for success in life."* **Dr. Joyce Brothers**

Jacket tips:

1. Ensure jacket is altered to fit impeccably.
2. Select small patterns or prints, as they are more business-like.
3. Keep your look consistent throughout the week.
4. Analyze and meet your clients' expectations of your image.

5. When in doubt, err on the more formal/conservative.
6. The jacket should be the mainstay and anchor for our business wardrobe. It keeps our business look business-like and still gives us flexibility when meeting clients or prospective employers. When you're well-dressed, you feel confident, and your clients notice and feel confident in you.

This purchase in your business attire will give you a good return on your investment.

Challenge: Have you objectively looked at yourself in the mirror lately? What do you see? Do you see a sales professional whose attire reinforces a personal commitment to delivering the best service and expertise to your customers?

Ask your colleagues or manager to rate you on the following:

1. Are your shoes shined and in good repair?
2. Are your clothes clean, co-coordinated, and pressed?
3. Is your hair clean and an appropriate length and cut for you?
4. Does your overall appearance denote professionalism and being prepared?
5. What needs to change to ensure you present a *professional* image?

PRO-tip: Making a sales call
State your full name and company name upfront.

Why? Research shows, important people state their full name. When you do this, it helps command respect.

You control the conversations by not having the prospective client ask, "Who is this?" The person who asks the questions controls the conversation. You as the professional want to lead not follow.

Rules of Value-Added Selling and Service

Customer satisfaction is relative to your actual or perceived performance and their expectations.

Customer satisfaction is a very subjective thing to measure. It really is a matter of perception and experience. If you meet or exceed the *'unsaid – unwritten'* expectations of your customers their perception will be a positive one. Fail to meet these expectations, and you will find them less than satisfied or happy with you. One method to make sure you meet or beat these *'unsaid —unwritten'* expectations is to do some research.

Often, within an industry there are certain expectations, which serve as the norm. Make sure you know what they are and use them as the bottom line in your service and performance. If you want to succeed in gaining their repeat business and loyalty, make sure you go well past the *'normal'* expectations.

There is some business you don't want – but you do want every opportunity to explore the potential to do business.

When you first start in sales or start a business, you want to deal with everyone. This works for the short-term, but not over the long term. Hard as it seems, you need to fire some clients if the business they bring in is not profitable to you or your company. Studies have shown that on average, 80% of your business will be generated from 20% of your customers. Yet many sales staff invest their time in those clients, who will bring the lowest return on their investment.

Your Price is TOO High!

Compared to what?

Be prepared to answer

© 2007 Bob Hooey, www.SecretSellingTips.com

You'll run into these two objections more often when you are not having a sales conversation with the right prospective client.

Additionally, trying to be *'all things to all people'* is a sure-fire way to go broke. You cannot effectively sell, service, or supply everyone. You need to decide early on what business you are in, and what you can provide *'profitably'* to your customers. You can't service them if you're no longer in business. Sales and its built-in customer service is a long-term investment in your business.

Key: Not all customers are valid targets for a value-added effort.

Point to Ponder: *"We are generally the better persuaded by the reasons we discover ourselves than by those given to us by others." Blaise Pascal*

As you develop your sales, decide which customers you can service profitably.

Profit is not a bad word – it is the lifeline of your business. It is the differential between having a 'job' or hobby, and a sales career. As you become increasingly clear on what business you are in and what you can profitably provide in the marketplace, you will be able to better target and serve your customers.

Selling when you are not able to do so profitably or service in a cost-effective way will lead to a loss of potential to build your business. You can't invest your profits in expanding your business if you haven't earned any.

Price is less important when the relationship between the buyer and the seller is stronger.

Think about your own shopping or buying experiences:

- Other than for convenience or disposable goods, where do you shop on a regular basis? Why?
- Would you drive across town to save a few dollars?
- How often would you continue to deal with that company or salesperson even if they are a bit higher in price? Why is that?

When the value of the product and its support and service are evident, and there is a strong relationship built on understanding and trust, people tend to be loyal and continue dealing with you.

Ask yourself:
- Would you agree that often it is the way you are treated that makes a big difference?
- Would you also agree that often it is the small details than make the difference?
- How can you develop this type of relationship with your customers?
- What would have to change to make it work in your situation?

Challenge: How can you apply the lessons learned from your own shopping experience in better taking care of your potential and existing customers?

PRO-tip: …it's my duty to show you! Part two

For several years, in the 80's, I was a sales rep for several eastern Canadian fabric manufactures and importers travelling Alberta and parts of BC.

Twice yearly, I would make appointments to show the new lines to fabric store owners and suggest purchases for their clientele. One thing I learned was to *not* overload or oversell them. I saw where other reps had short sightedly done this in one season only to come the next and see much of their wares sitting unsold on the shelves. Needless to say, they didn't make big sales in subsequent seasons. Mid seasons, I touched base with them with new ideas and reminders that we carried their staples.

I *strategically* worked to 'serve them best' by only selling them items we were certain would sell and make sure they were not left with excessive, expensive old stock. This allowed us to more than double our sales moving well into the million-dollar levels in subsequent years.

© **Bob 'Idea Man' Hooey**, www.ideaman.net *Excerpt from Thinking Beyond the FIRST Sale*

Sales Success Secrets

Creating Repeat Buyers for Salespeople

For most businesses, the cost of getting a *'new'* customer is about 10 times greater than getting a re-order from an *'existing'* customer. Being successful in the sales game means making the best of your time and increasing the overall volume of *'profitable'* sales you bring into your company.

Yet most salespeople miss the more *'profitable'* long-term relationships with their current clientele and spend their time prospecting and attempting to close *'new'* clients. Okay, many of them also spend time in non-sales activities too!

Point to Ponder: *New clients provide growth; mining existing clients provides profit and sustained long-term growth.*

In this chapter we investigate why and how you should act if creating repeat buyers is your goal. We'll outline some techniques and tools field-proven by North America's sales professionals that can be profitably applied when you return to your sales environment.

In business there are **three major methods to increase your business:**
1) **Increase the *'number'* of clients;**
2) **Increase the average *'size'* of the sale per client;**
3) **Increase the *'number of times'* a client returns and buys again.**

This book focuses on providing proven tools and techniques to help you primarily in the second two methods. It helps you pre-qualify and evaluate your prospects by evaluating their life-time-value as a client.

Focusing on the second two methods and taking care of your current clients by providing *'exceptional customer satisfaction'* will also generate new clients.

People love to share a good experience and will start 'selling' or referring you to their friends and business associates.

50

It will help you develop a simple ABC account management system focused on increased sales and overall account growth. Having a system in place will allow you to focus your energies for maximum potential on the clients who will *'profitably'* grow with you.

According to a Boston based consulting firm the average Fortune 500 Company could *'instantly'* double its revenue growth rate with a 5 % increase in client/customer retention.

They further stated that a small to midsize company could double its profits in ten years by simply increasing its customer retention rate by 5%. Interesting parallel in process, timeline, and results for small, midsize, and large firm's profitability.

People buy for various reasons and buying has an emotional attachment. Knowing why people buy will allow you to position, or re-position yourself and your company to provide additional products and services over an extended time.

Out of sight, out of mind. Many clients simply get ignored, forget who they bought their product or service from, and drift away. Create a systematic process that keeps you in the top-of-mind position as a value-added resource to your clients. Remind them of their importance and learn ways to creatively touch base and sell them again and again. What are you doing to help them remember you?

Customer service is a solid foundation for continued relationship and increased long-term sales potential. Keep them satisfied and they will keep buying from you and referring you. A simple point, but often missed by *'average'* companies and sales staff.

According to a study (6000 customers)
- 95% were willing to be repeat customers based on receiving *'excellent'* service and products,
- 62% after receiving *'good'* service (acceptable but not impressive),
- 7% based on receiving only *'fair'* service and products,
- None from those who received *'poor'* goods or services.

Do the math! Another hint: satisfied clients become fans and champions for you and your firm and can dynamically increase your overall sales.

The impact of treating our best clients/customers well is staggering. Most of us shop for groceries on a regular basis, so you might find this of interest. In a Harvard Business Review article, **Alan Grant** and **Leonard Schlesinger** wrote:

"Given the fixed cost structure of a grocery store, the contribution margin from each dollar spent by a customer can earn 10 times the store's net profit margin. Thus, the company found that even small improvements in any one of the customer behaviours led to very significant profitability gains. Expanding the customer base by two percent with primary shoppers, for example, would increase the store's profitability by more than 45%. Converting just 200 secondary customers into primary shoppers would increase the profitability by 20 per cent. Persuading every customer to substitute two store-brand items for two national-brand items each time they visited the store would increase profitability by 55 percent."

There is a lesson for each of us as sales professionals in taking care of our primary customers and mining our secondary customers for repeat business. In both cases the increase in profits underscores and pays handsomely for the effort in doing so.

And yet according to *American Demographics*, grocery shopping is the second less popular activity of 22 daily tasks. It rates only ahead of going to the dentist. People spend the equivalent of two-and-a-half (work) weeks shopping each year, not including the time spend in transit. A study by the *National Retail Federation* uncovered nearly half of those surveyed feel shopping is a hassle to be avoided. A staggering 74% of men and 58% of women reported they would sometimes walk out of a store because they felt the wait is too long. And guess who gets the express lines *(the ones with the smallest number of purchases in their basket)* …hmmm!

Perhaps this is what leads the creation of on-line shopping and personal shopping services as viable and profitable alternatives.

What are the frustrations facing your clients in dealing with you and what specific remedies are you working to implement to offset them? How are you making dealing with you a more pleasant, hassle-free experience?

How can you make yourself and your company easier to do business with for you customers?

People have choices. With the explosion of Internet business alternatives, people have more choice than ever in our history. This creates challenges and opportunities for those of us who are sales professionals.

- What are you doing to ensure your availability and accessibility to your customers? How accessible are you?
- How have you harnessed the Internet to help you serve them better and give them service or information along side your personal attention?

Investing your time wisely. Creating more face-to-face time for the sales and marketing process will give you an amazing return on your investment (ROI).

Acquire some simple priority management skills that can free up to 2 hours per day to contact and serve your existing clients, and of course capture some new profitable ones along the way.

Challenge: Before we dive into more ideas, let's take a moment and brainstorm some ideas or reasons why '*you*' would like to find ways to create repeat buyers for your firm.

Explore '*why*' you would like to create add-on orders or have customers thank you for up-sell them. Jot down your thoughts, and the ideas generated from discussions with your fellow participants.

Sales Success Secrets

Field-Proven Tips to Increase Your Sales Income

Most of us in the sales profession are driven by goals. One goal is finding ways to increase our sales income and reduce our time demands in doing so. **My Sales Success Secrets goal for you: work smarter and make *much* more money!** We want to see your big, outrageous goal become a reality, don't we?

Is this an achievable goal?

YES! One of the ways of doing that is in converting your *one-time* customers into regular clients who come back again and again to buy from you.

My Secret Selling goal for you: work smarter and make *much* more money!

© 2007 Bob Hooey, www.SecretSellingTips.com

Better yet, they bring their friends, too. This is one of the best ways of increasing your income.

Finding ways to get your potential and current customers to *buy in larger quantities* is a valuable goal. And of course, finding new customers and getting *qualified* leads and referrals from existing customers is a valid goal, too. Valuable as well, I might add!

Here are some practical tips, which when applied, allow you to hone your sales skills and accomplish all these goals.

Become an Avid Reader (Sales leaders are more often readers!)

There are essentially only two ways to learn new things. One is through your own experience; the other, more effective way, is *leveraged learning* through other people's experiences.

Sales professionals are often readers in search of new ideas, methods, and training materials to equip themselves to better prospect, qualify, sell, and then successfully build long-term customer relationships. What *profitable* ideas have you learned from someone else lately?

Point to Ponder: *"People who take risks are the people you will lose against."* **John Sculley**

Have Fun Selling!

You spend more time working than any other activity in your life, so why not enjoy the time you invest in the Sales process? Don't *just* think of Sales as work. View it as enjoyable as any of your favorite family, leisure, or sports activities. When you get good at it – that's what happens anyway. People *'earn'* and *'learn'* more in times of enjoyment!

Attend Training Seminars to Hone Your Sales Skills

Don't wait on your company to lead or train you! Invest in yourself and your sales future. There is no better way to learn a skill than attending a seminar or sales boot camp by street smart, successful sales experts, either live or on-line. This is a true success secret from the sales superstars!

Delegate

Most of your sales time should be spent meeting with prospects and customers – not just doing administrative *busy* work! Follow up and paperwork are a solid part of the Sales process but don't allow yourself to get bogged down in this area.

Subscribe to Informative On-line Newsletters

Subscribe to successful *'sales* and motivational newsletters to keep up to date on hot new techniques and ideas for your business. There's nothing better than getting a regular helping of fresh hot new ideas and perspectives from experts on sales. Invest time to read and reflect.

Have the Right Attitude about Sales

The right attitude about sales will carry you through, regardless of what challenges or obstacles are thrown in your way. Learning to view prospecting as natural, and sales as an ongoing event, will make you a sales champion. It will also make you wealthy! Building solid relationships which generate repeat business begins with the right attitudes.

Don't Make Excuses for Your Lack of Sales Success

Under-performers love to have a scapegoat to blame for their failures or lack of achievement. If you talk to them, it is always something – the economy, the competition, the product, or the price… anything other than themselves and their lack of commitment or performance. As a successful salesperson, you realize that your success, or lack of it, is totally, 100% your responsibility! Take personal leadership of your Sales role and take corrective steps to add to your skills and succeed.

Welcome Your Mistakes as Learning Opportunities

Everyone makes mistakes. Successful sales professionals realize mistakes are a part of their learning curve and maximize the lesson from each one. *"Next time I will do _____"* is their professional response to a *new* learning experience. Don't spend your time worrying or feeling victimized by mistakes. Instead spend 99% of your time thinking about a solution, as do the sales superstars! It works!

Challenge: How many of these tips are you presently using? Do you see any that could be initiated immediately? Well, what are you waiting for…?

"Establishing trust is better than any sales technique."
Mike Puglia

Creating Fans and Champions – Getting Your Customers to Sell For You

Over the years I have discovered, quite by accident, that my best investment to increase my sales and build my business was in taking *'very good care'* of my current clients/customers.

When they are happy and more than satisfied with my products or service, they will talk about me to their friends, family, and colleagues. Isn't that what you really want in your sales journey?

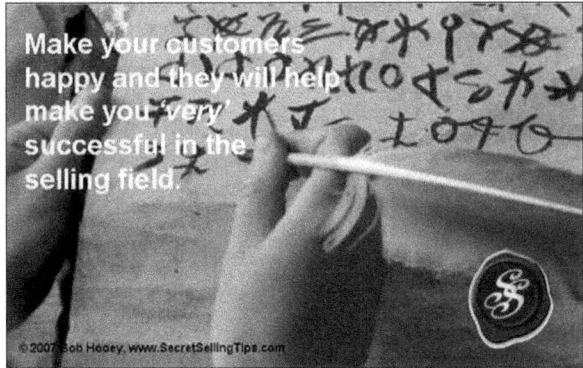

Make your customers happy and they will help make you *'very'* successful in the selling field.

© 2007 Bob Hooey, www.SecretSellingTips.com

Some will even go the extra mile to becoming fans or champions and start *firmly* telling their friends and colleagues that they *'must'* deal with me if they want the best value or service. Wow!

Is your intention to become or remain a million-dollar sales writer and build a profitable career in sales? Applying these tips and techniques will be beneficial in your quest for sales success.

Go the extra mile – *inspired* action to separate yourself from your competition

One effective activity in building loyalty and turning customers into repeat buyers, raving fans, and champions of your service or business is to go the extra mile. By this I mean, doing more than would be **normal** to help them achieve the success or satisfaction they wanted.

- Have you ever experienced having someone going way past your expectations in what would normally be included in your purchase?
- Did it catch your attention and make you take notice? Did you talk about it?
- How can you do this with your customers?

Point to Ponder: *"Real excellence does not come cheaply. A certain price must be paid in terms of practice, patience, and persistence – natural ability, notwithstanding."* Stephen R. Covey

Do the unexpected – truly amaze them

Sales professionals and their companies have the opportunity to build amazing relationships and repeat business. Yet so few are successful.

- How many times have you been positively surprised in dealing with a salesperson or company?
- They gave you more than you expected, or did something you thought would be an extra?
- How did you feel?
- How can you do that in your sales efforts and business?
- Are there some small value-added areas or 'extras' that you can incorporate into your service or product mix?

Follow up for complete satisfaction – a key part of the sales process

One of the areas for growth in providing real value-added service is in the follow-up or follow-through. Sadly, too many salespeople miss a great opportunity to build profitable long-term relationships simply by not following up.

Customer service is pro-active and deals with the little *'adjustments'* before they become major irritants. The very thing that can turn customers into loyal fans and we're afraid to do it. How will you incorporate this area of ***exceptional*** customer service into your sales process?

Keep in touch – top of mind means additional sales and business

Part of building a positive relationship and converting customers into loyal fans and enthusiastic champions can be as simple as keeping in contact. How can you build in an easily maintained system to allow you to track your customers? How will you find ways to keep in touch? What commitment will you make to ensure it gets done?

- Are there any opportunities you've missed to establish this mutually beneficial type of customer relationship?
- Can you see where you may be able to reconnect and recapture this lost business?
- Can you think about areas you can change to ensure you connect and create long term, mutually profitable, relationships with potential or current customers?

Challenge: Take a moment and think of some other ways that will help you build those relationships that turn your customers into repeat buyers, fans, and champions.

Talk with your sales team about how you can ensure you don't miss any new opportunities. It is never too late to do what is right and to ask for a second chance. Keep in mind the potential lifetime value potential of your customers and treat them accordingly.

PRO-tip: Never lead with your business card when making a face-to-face cold call. Reach out, shake hands with the receptionist, introduce yourself and ask for his or her name. Comment on something unique in the office and then say, *"I need your help."* When they answer, state why you are there. The objective is **not** to look like every other salesperson that comes in the office.

© **Joe Bonura**, *www.bonura.com*

Henry Ford said, ***"Before everything else, being ready is the Secret of Success!"***

Customer Service Redefined as a Sales Tool

'Is there some *new* service or *additional* product I should be providing that would make *'your'* shopping experience easier, more rewarding or user friendly?' Just one of the two questions you need to ask yourself and your customers on a frequent basis.

Remember, **if you aren't asking these questions – your competitors are!**

Here are some tools which will help you keep and expand your market edge; tools to keep your customers happy and coming back for more.

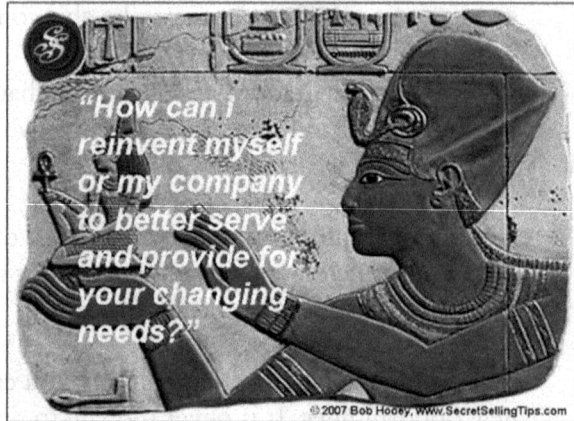

"How can I reinvent myself or my company to better serve and provide for your changing needs?"

© 2007 Bob Hooey, www.SecretSellingTips.com

Each of these tools provides a *'valid'* reason to touch base with existing clients, and a chance to do additional, repeat business. Why not invest time to develop an account management system that incorporates one or more of these tools?

It may provide insights on how to retain, retrain, or remain a *trusted advisor* to their family or a long-term supplier or vendor of choice. As a Sales professional, *each* of these can easily be done (by you) to keep in touch and build your customer relationships.

Point to Ponder: *Remember, out of sight leads to out of mind. This leads to out of the running for repeat business and referrals, which are the lifeblood of the sales professional.*

Customer surveys. Checking in on a regular basis to ask a *'few key'* questions (*never more than 5*) can work wonders. Look at the survey answers for tips to make your sales efforts and business more responsive and profitable. This might be something you co-create with your fellow sales team members and send out to current customers from time to time. Could be something as simple as a post card they can mail back or design and send a simple email (*you are capturing their address, right?*)

Telephone or email polls. A quick phone call or email to selected customers might be enough to keep you informed and current as to how well you are doing. How about actually contacting them a month or so after you've delivered your service or product to see how it is going and how the clients are enjoying it. This is a great use of your down time and if you systematically check in with your customers you remain top of mind as well. You might have an email survey for this same purpose.

Service calls. These are a neglected form of information as to the true satisfaction of your customers and the serviceability of your products. Make your service team part of your information gathering team and apply what you learn to make your business better.

Delivery teams. These team members are often the last contact with the clients. Get to know them and ask them to share their observations with you. They see and hear things that your sales teams can use to help customers in the future. Tap into this unused resource.

Focus groups. Invest some time and invite a few of your *best* customers to sit down and discuss honestly what you offer and what you deliver. Put your ego on hold and listen carefully, as they give you a truly valuable gift – a gift that will help you grow and succeed.

Product sampling or demonstration. What a great way to find out what your customers want and what you can provide professionally and profitably. You might also ask good clients to drop in for a visit to check out a new product.

Offer to buy them a coffee or have a coupon for a treat you can give them for helping you.

Web site feedback. This is emerging as a great way to allow your clients to tell you how you are doing, what they like, what they don't like and what they would like from you.

Ask your website team what kind of comments or reaction they are getting and what areas and products are getting the most visits. Many shoppers are going online to do research perhaps on you and your company site before they come in to see you. Knowing what they've looked at will help you prepare and focus your own learning to better serve them.

Challenge: Discuss how you and your fellow sales team members can incorporate one or more of these tools in your current personal or store marketing and sales strategies.

If you have an idea to share, send it to me at: bhooey@mcsnet.ca

Invest in your sales and business future by asking good questions and then acting on the responses your customers give you. This might just be the competitive 'sales' edge you need as you continue to navigate the turbulent and volatile field of business in 21st Century.

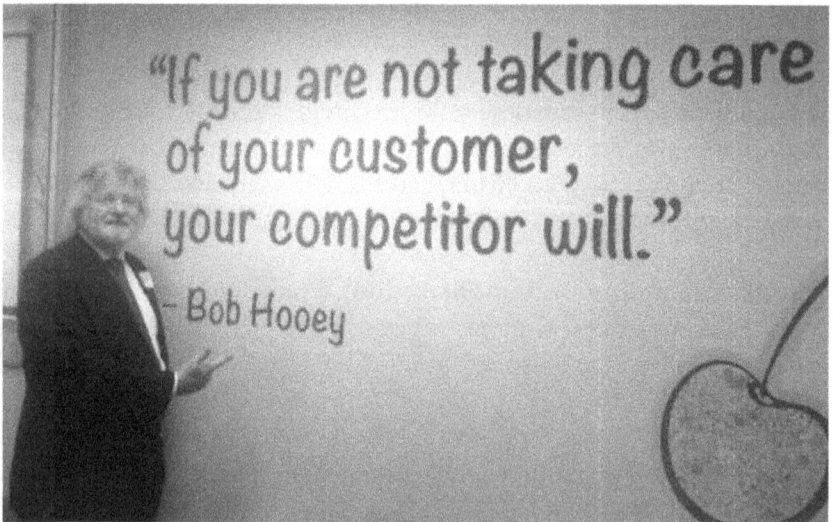

Customer service is the motivation behind the sales process. This wall *(pictured above)* is the 'Hooey' training room in Johannesburg, South Africa.

Master, Who Is My Customer?

Many years ago, a young servant (salesman) came to his master and enquired of him how he should be successful in business. The wise master said, *'By taking care of the real needs and providing true value for your customers.'* The young servant replied, *'But Master, who is my customer?'*

This parable, adapted from my Sunday school days, illustrates the confusion we all too often have in work or business. *'Who is your customer?'* I would contend that we have both *'internal'* and *'external'* customers.

Both are important to your long-term sales success! Without satisfied external customers you have no business, and without involved and committed internal customers you will lose it to your competition.

External customers are those who would do or continue to do business with us and allow us to make a profit.

- Why would it be important to make sure we take care of the needs of our external customers?
- What can you do to ensure they are taken care of effectively and completely?

Internal customers are those who assist us in making our business successful by playing a part or supplying something we need to be successful ... our management team, co-workers, suppliers, and sub-contractors.

- The same question on taking care of our internal customer's needs requires a bit more thought, doesn't it?

- Why would it make sense to take care of those who work alongside you in your business, or do part of the sales, delivery, service, or installation process? To your customer, **'they' are the company** and each time they encounter one of them, your reputation and referral factor is on the line.

Why would it make sense to take care of those who supply you with products or services? None of us work in isolation, do we?

Challenge: Give some thought to the following questions.

- In a pinch when you *'just gotta have it'* - whom do you think your suppliers will help? Perhaps the person who has *consistently* treated them well?
- Why would that be? (skill testing question here)
- What can you do to build a relationship that returns a positive response?
- What are you committed to doing to increase your effectiveness in serving your external customers and internal customers alike?
- When will you implement it? Act soon to protect your career investment!

Point to Ponder: *Smart businesses and career-focused employees learn to focus their energies on making sure the internal and external customers are taken care of and satisfied.*

This is the secret of building a super successful business or productive career!

PRO-tip: While in the kitchen design business, I tracked my leads. Surprisingly enough, I found we generated 3-5 referrals from happy clients within the first 2-years. That reinforced my attention to detail and making sure each client was fully satisfied with our work. It also encouraged me to follow up and keep in touch with them. How are you doing with your retention and referrals?

Qualifying 'Continued' As a Crucial Step in Your Sales Success

Your sales success can *hinge* on how well you know your competition, your customer, and your capacity to provide solutions that capture their confidence and their business.

Sales are *frequently* lost when getting to know the customer, their needs, and wants is rushed or ignored in your haste to capture the sale. The secret to becoming a H-U-G-E success in sales is to have a comfortable, proven process. A personalized, systematic, step-by-step process you *actually* follow day-in and day-out. Create and refine your qualifying as a key part of your sales success process and it's easy to increase your revenues and profits without working more hours.

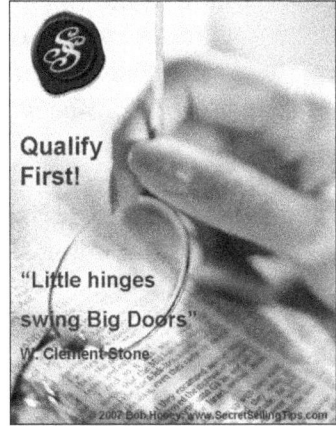

Qualify First!

"Little hinges swing Big Doors"
W. Clement Stone

© 2007 Bob Hooey, www.SecretSellingTips.com

Investing time to in dig deeper as part of the sales process achieves two essential things:

- It improves your chance of getting the eventual order or sale by building solid foundations to reveal and help solve your customer's problems.
- It sets the stage for a long-term mutually beneficial relationship as well as enhanced customer referrals and repeat business.

Point to Ponder: *"Make your products easier to buy than your competition or you will find your customers buying from them." Mark Cuban*

You might want to know:

- **What is the client/customer's problem or opportunity you can solve?** You and the customer are talking about something. He or she is visiting your store or asking you to put a proposal together for some specific reason. What is the problem or opportunity? If there's no problem (challenge, opportunity, supply need, i.e., product or service under consideration), there's no sale.

- **What is the financial impact of the customer's problem?** How is the problem impacting them? Is there a way to *quantify* the dollar amount or value of the problem? It must either be costing him money, wasting his time, or is just inconvenient. Perhaps it is a choice to *improve* or beautify a living space? How will it fit, how will it look, how will it feel? When you're able to get the customer to tell you how this is impacting their situation, your probability of closing the sale dramatically increases.

- **Who is the decision maker?** Are you talking with the decision maker? If not, it's often a complete and total waste of your time! In retail, who is your customer? Make sure you are talking to them.

- **What is the decision-making process?** You need to know how your customer will decide to hire, engage your services, or buy from you. It's always enlightening when you ask, 'What criteria will you use to make your decision?' Nice to know if they are shopping your competition too. Often, the client or customer doesn't have a clue or is able to articulate it. Their answer enables you to ask more questions as you identify and define what is 'really' important to the customer.

- **Where is the sense of urgency?** If there's no sense of urgency nothing's going to happen! Why do they need to buy something? And why do they need to do it now? If you know the answer, you've probably got yourself a sale. If you don't, nothing's going to happen. Is it an advertised sales item or limited time offering?

- **Ask For The Sale!** It's OK to ask for the sale at any stage in the Sales process. In fact, that is your job! Using a soft or trial close is a great qualifying tool to check in with your customer. It can be fun to see what happens when you say something like this:

- When do you want this delivered?
- Would you like to sign this agreement (contract, purchase order)?
- Please sign here.

Your customer's reaction will tell you a lot about where the sales conversation, and your sales opportunity, is going.

Remember, manage your probe time.

Discuss and explore your potential customers' business facts or potential choices: timing, objectives, specifications, etc. quickly. Invest more of your time – 75 to 80% discussing their problems or challenges in reaching their goals, how these problems impact them, the cost of doing nothing, the rewards of acting, or resolving the challenge, and the options they've considered so far. (Qualifying) Don't skimp in establishing a relationship or demonstrating your understanding of their needs, criteria, decision process or ability to act.

One last hint: Don't be afraid to invest time educating your potential clients/customers on why you provide better services, products or how they work. That too is part of the pre-qualifying process and a great way to demonstrate your expertise and professionalism as well.

When I worked with Jack Horner designing kitchens, he would take extra time to demonstrate the extra quality he built into each cabinet. I asked him why he did that when so many were just looking? He said, 'when they go visit the next cabinet shop, they will ask questions about their quality and warrantees. Often, they will come back when they realize there is a valid reason why we offer a 5-year guaranty when the norm is only 1-year.'

Challenge: How much of your time is spent pre-qualifying and getting to know your clients/customers and their shopping needs? What needs to change?

How To Turn Your Sales Into Repeat Business

Most sales driven organizations are *'so'* preoccupied getting *'new'* customers; they pay little attention to their existing customers. It is an *expensive* mistake when you let them `slip away'` as you have essentially just wasted your money and your efforts in getting them in the first place.

By investing time in generating repeat business from your *existing* clients **you and your company will reap the following benefits:**

- You save on advertising costs to get a new customer in the first place.
- They need your product/service, so they are your *continuing* target market.
- You can have a more effective mail out for follow up contacts and add-on sales.
- You can ask them what they want and then you seek to satisfy them.
- If they are happy with you and your organization, they will tell others - the power of word-of-mouth.
- You can make your *existing* customers an offer which can include their friends and colleagues.

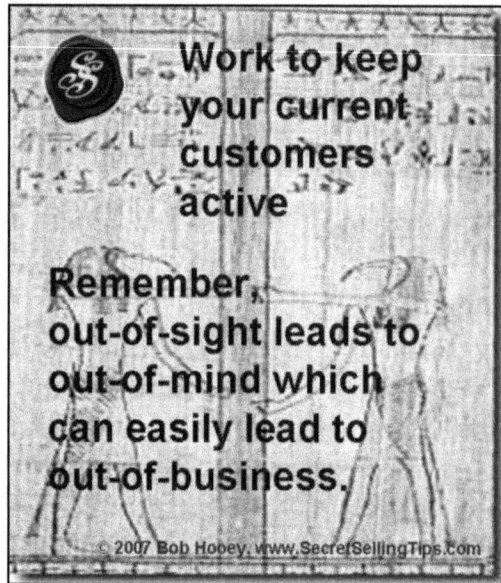

Work to keep your current customers active

Remember, out-of-sight leads to out-of-mind which can easily lead to out-of-business.

© 2007 Bob Hooey. www.SecretSellingTips.com

Because you've already spent a substantial portion of advertising money on attracting a new client/customer; it makes good sense *(and dollars too)* to work at keeping that customer once they have made a purchase.

Point to Ponder: *"I think there is something more important than believing: Action! The world is full of dreamers, there aren't enough who will move ahead and begin to take concrete steps to actualize their vision."* **W. Clement Stone**

For your sales career to grow and be successful, you need to develop a *growing* relationship with your existing customers, so they understand that your business is looking after them. If they have already bought from you then they *are* your target market – so don't forget them. Chances are if they are happy with your business, they will buy from you again. They just need reminding of the benefits that your business can offer them and their friends and family. Remind them you are still here!

Remember, out-of-sight leads to out-of-mind which can lead to out-of-business.

What does it cost your firm to acquire a 'new' customer?

Ask your Chief Financial Officer or Sales Manager for this figure: $_____ Often that figure is 5-10 times the cost of keeping a *current* customer and expanding the business they do with you.

Challenge: To help you measure your potential to secure repeat business, ask yourself these questions:

1. How good is your personal and your company's customer service?

2. Have you got systems in place to ensure consistency of service and product development?

3. Are you happy with your image – are you relaying the 'right' message?

4. What does your organisation do for customers that your competitors are not doing?

5. Do you make the most of the testimonials from your satisfied customers to keep the momentum going?

6. Do you have promotional activities in place which targets your existing customers, and which makes them 'feel' valued and special?

7. Do you survey your existing customers to help improve your product or service to them?

So, how did you rate?

Believe it or not there's much more to know when it comes to maximizing your sales potential for repeat business. Keep your existing customers coming back for more and getting them to *'spread the word'* about your business.

For your Sales Success Secrets library

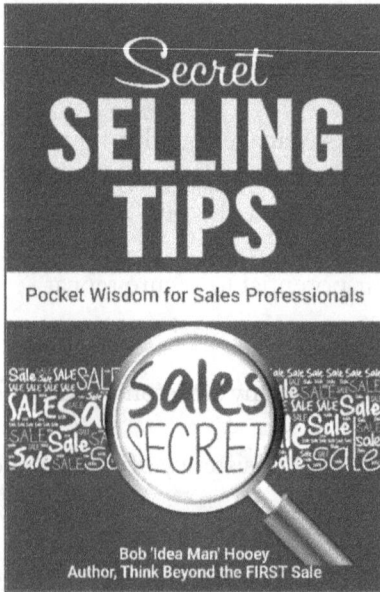

My purpose in creating this mini-motivational book is to provide you with a positive daily dose of motivation or food for thought. A thought which will help you focus your mind on the positive as well as on looking for new opportunities to grow, to hone your skills, to gain expertise and to be better equipped to serve and sell prospective customers. A thought which will remind you to leverage your efforts in building long-term mutually beneficial relationships which generate both profitable repeat business and qualified referrals. "At its essence, success in any selling field is a 'mental' game."

www.amazon.com/dp/B08P1M1X8T?ref_=pe_3052080_397514860

Managers: Why not buy one for your whole sales team. Hire Bob!

*"There is **no better way to become a leading sales professional** than reading and acting on these Secret Selling Tips."* **Kim Yost,** *former President and CEO, The Brick Group*

The Influential Power of One Person With a Purpose

Each of us has the opportunity to become amazing *centers of influence* in our roles as sales professionals, as demonstrated by the unique ways we interact and treat our customers. This can be a sense of *professionalism on purpose* and can literally explode your career and Sales success. You have the power to connect with your customers in unique ways and to help transform them into long term fans and champions of both yourself and your store.

Earlier, I mentioned the story of **Johnny the Bagger** from my friend and contagious cheerleader, **Barbara Glanz.**

Barbara: I also give to each audience member a small card that says on the front, **'Thank you for CARE-ing'** with a picture of a CARE package. On the back it says, **'Spread Contagious Enthusiasm - Pass It Along,'** and I ask them to give the card to someone who makes a difference in their life within the next 48 hours. After sharing several other examples of how people add their unique spirit to their jobs, my challenge to them is to get their creative juices going to come up with their OWN creative personal signature.

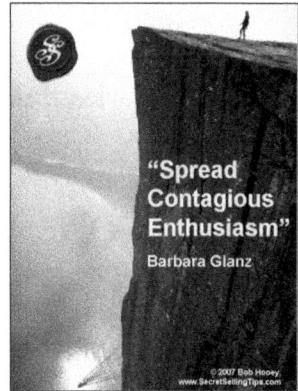

"Spread Contagious Enthusiasm"

Barbara Glanz

© 2007 Bob Hooey, www.SecretSellingTips.com

Here is an excerpt from that story for your consideration *(used with her kind permission).*

About 3 weeks after I had spoken to [a group of] supermarket employees, my phone rang late one afternoon. The person on the line told me that his name was Johnny and that he was a bagger in one of the stores. He also told me that he was a Down's Syndrome person. He said, *'Barbara, I liked what you said!'* Then he went on to tell me how when he'd gone home that night, he asked his Dad to teach him to use the computer.

He said they set it up in three columns, and each night now when he goes home, he finds a *'thought for the day.'* He said, *"If I can't find one, I like, I think one up!"* Then he and his Dad type it into the computer, nine times on a page, and they print out at least 200 pages each night.

Then he cuts them out, signs his name on the back of each one, and the next day *'with flourish,'* **he puts a thought for the day in each person's groceries he bags**, adding his own personal signature in a heartwarming, fun, and creative way.

One month later the manager of the store called me. He said, *"Barbara, you won't believe what happened today. When I went out on the floor this morning, the line at Johnny's checkout was* three times longer *than any other line!"* He said, *"I went ballistic, yelling, 'Get more lanes open! Get more people out here,"* but the customers said, *"No no! We want to be in Johnny's lane -- we want the thought for the day!"*

He said one woman even came up and told him, *"I only used to shop once a week, and now I come in every time I go by because I want the thought for the day!"* (Imagine what that does to the bottom line?) He ended by saying, *"Who do you think is the* **most important person** *in our whole store?"* Johnny, of course!

Point to Ponder: *"Be kind. Everyone you meet is carrying something." Barbara Glanz*

Three months later he called me again, *"***You and Johnny have transformed our store!** *Now in the floral department when they have a broken flower or an unused corsage, they go out on the floor and find an elderly woman or a little girl and pin it on them. One of our meat packers loves Snoopy, so he bought 50,000 Snoopy stickers, and each time he packages a piece of meat, he puts a Snoopy sticker on it.* **We** *are having so much fun, and our* **customers** *are having so much fun!"* THAT is spirit in the workplace!

It never ceases to amaze me whenever I tell this beautiful story how little it takes to regenerate the spirit in a workplace. Johnny took what many of us might consider to be a not very important job and he made it important by adding his own personal signature.

My challenge and yours – *if young Johnny can do it, there is no reason why each one of us can't do it, too!*

Imagine the new spirit of self-esteem, commitment, and fun which could permeate our places of work if we each, like Johnny, found a way to add our special, unique touch to our job!

Challenge: Give some thought to something you can do that helps create a *'unique'* experience for your customers. If Johnny can do it, why can't you?

- This would be a great opportunity to brainstorm ideas with fellow sales professionals.
- Look for ways to add your unique personal touch and personality to your sales.

PRO-tips: Strategies for beginners
- Know your product or service completely.
- Understand your prospective clients' pain points.
- Do your research on your prospective client in advance.
- Always follow up.
- Use each rejection as an opportunity to learn and grow.

More seasoned sales pros:
- Manage your time wisely for better results.
- Leverage technology to enhance productivity.
- Understand your prospect's role in the organization.
- Never stop prospecting for new clients.
- Work on your ability to handle objections.
- Leverage empathy to enhance connections.
- Quality focus instead of quantity.
- Build a sales process that is measurable and repeatable.
- Always be on the lookout for referrals.

Sales Success Secrets

Avoid 'Premature' Discounting

A number of years back, my wife and I were shopping at one of evening open markets while stopping in Hong Kong en-route to Australia.

I saw a crowded stall with a wide variety of colorful silk scarves. Wow!

Now, I normally wear scarves when I speak, and it has become a signature accessory for me. I am always on the lookout for new colors and shades to add to my on-stage collection.

I picked out one very vibrant shade of purple and asked her, how much?

> Premature discounting is *'unprofessional'* and costs you much more than *'just'* money.
>
> **It costs you sales success!**
>
> © 2007 Bob Hooey, www.SecretSellingTips.com

After I told the clerk that we wanted to take the scarf, the clerk violated one of the never-do principles of sales... she *volunteered* a discount!

Please note, I did not ask for a discount.

But, without blinking, she essentially gave us 25% off the retail price.

This prompted my curiosity. I wanted to see how much more I could get if I pushed a bit. I went into the role of the *reluctant* customer who is having second thoughts. I told her we wanted to look at some other stalls in the market before making my final decision. She responded by taking *another* 25% off. That's essentially a net 50% discount in less than 60 seconds! I was curious to see how far I could get her to go before she threw up her hands on me.

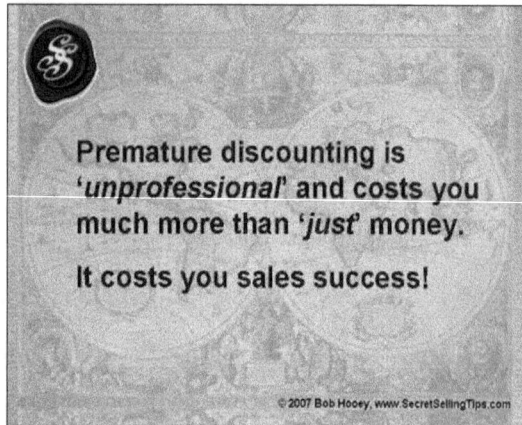

I continued to press her and, each time I stalled, offered an objection, or gave some indication that I may not be ready to make the decision, she sweetened the pot. I finally walked out of the booth with 13 delightful silks scarves for the equivalent of about $40 Canadian. Scarves of similar value that I had paid $20 plus 'each' for around the globe. Wow!

What is the lesson for us as salespeople? Never, ever, under any circumstances, volunteer a discount prematurely.

Point to Ponder: *"The more people understand the value of what they are doing, the more motivated they are to do it well. Similarly, the better they understand what their individual rewards will be, that is, 'what is in it for them,' the more motivated they will be."* **Dr. David Campbell**

This *all-too-common story reinforces the point that salespeople are often guilty of unnecessarily* bringing up price objections and discounting too early.

Too often, we are focused on the price of our products and services instead of focused on the value they bring to our customer's lives. Value is what creates the more dominant buying action in our customers. We need to be competitively priced in our marketplace but remember price is only one of the factors in perceived value. How about your service, selection, payment plans, deliveries and other factors that are in your tool kit to help your prospective customers?

Challenge: Mentally go back over your past dozen sales encounters where you ended up with a purchase. What did you do during the sales process?

- Did you bring up a discount or deal or did the customer?
- Did you sell for the full listed or advertised price or did you use an incentive to close the deal?

Avoid this *costly* mistake of falsely assuming that price is the *only* reason people use to make a buying decision. In fact, it is number 5 or 6 on their list. **Hint**: In negotiating, look for a trade off if there is a discount being discussed.

Customers Have Needs Too

If you are *serious* about building a successful sales career, based on solid foundations of *value-based* customer service, there are insights about your customers you may need to know. If you want your clients/customers to receive the *best contact* with you as well as want them to be positively impressed with your care and concern for them, read on.

People are unique!

Not *one* of us is the same. We *each* have different needs. When you meet or exceed those needs, your customers feel important and would want you to keep helping them.

There are some needs we all share or hold in common. Investing time to ensure you, as a sales professional, seriously address these needs will help build a solid relationship and a profitable, successful sales career.

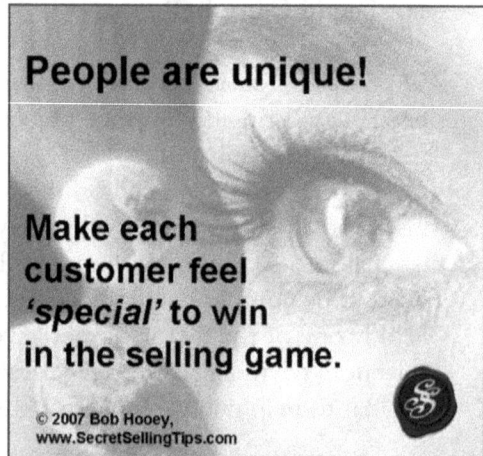

People are unique!

Make each customer feel 'special' to win in the selling game.

© 2007 Bob Hooey,
www.SecretSellingTips.com

Simply put, *you win in the sales game when you win with people*.

Here are some basic needs we all share:

- **Make '*me*' feel valued by you.** How do you accomplish this at present? Do you? What changes are needed for you to ensure your customers feel valued, *by you*?
- **Make '*me*' feel comfortable with you and not pressured.** Is this how they really feel? What needs to change or improve to meet this basic need and create this type of positive atmosphere when they visit your store? *'Serve not stalk,'* might be your motto here.

- **Give '_me_' your '_undivided_' attention. Wow!** This is a tough one, but can you do this? How do you discipline yourself so you can provide this _customer centered_ focus? Are there training or staffing tips that affect this area? Ask your manager for help on this one.

Point to Ponder: _"To become successful you must be a person of action. Merely to 'know' is not enough. It is necessary to both know and do."_ **Napoleon Hill**

- **Don't judge 'ME' by your perception of my ability to afford what you sell.** How many times have you caught yourself making this _un-founded and often wrong_ judgment? Each person coming into your place of business is a potential customer – if not now, perhaps later. **Explore their needs and treat them all special!** Invite them to visit in the future.

- **Focus more on 'ME' than your work schedules activities, rules, or personal life.** This is a sales and business killer. How often have you favored your store 'policies' rather than responding or dealing with a customer's _legitimate_ needs or problem? How often have you allowed your personal life or fellow sales staff to distract you from _fully_ serving your customers? What needs to change or improve in this area?

- **Don't ignore '_ME_' for someone who appears to be a '_better_' prospect.** Have you ever been on the receiving end of this one? How did it feel? Ouch! What can you do to ensure none of your customers' (_especially seniors and kids_) feels this way?

Just a few areas where being _sensitive_ to the real needs of your customers will help you create and build a good solid long-term relationship. This will help bring them back to buy from you again and again.

Being sensitive will also nudge them along the path to becoming your staunchest fans and champions with their friends, colleagues and family.

Challenge: Invest a few moments and reflect on your last dozen or so customer interactions.

- How well did you do in relation to these points?
- Would you give yourself a passing score?

Ask your sales team to help you *objectively* view your performance.

- Are there areas where you know you need to improve?
- What specific steps can you take to ensure you incorporate this sensitivity and focus into your sales activities and conversations?

For your Sales Success Secrets library

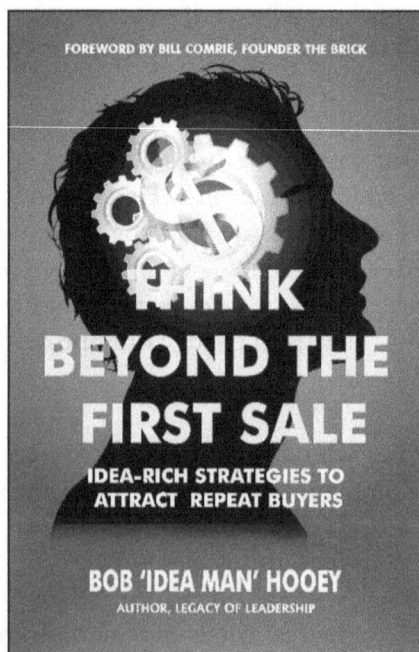

"This fast-moving, practical book, loaded with proven techniques and strategies, shows you how to make more sales, faster and easier, and how to keep those customers for life." **Brian Tracy**

Explore proven ways to enhance your business, increase your sales, and build long-term client relationships. Learn how to: Increase the number of clients; Increase the average size of the sale per client; Increase the frequency at which a client returns to buy again. **Top sales professionals** know and focus their energies on the most important aspects of the selling process – acquiring, serving, and keeping their clients.

Visit: www.amazon.com/Think-Beyond-FIRST-Sale-strategies/dp/1543294294/ to get your personal copy

PS: You can hire Bob to help educate your sales teams in this value-added concept. bhooey@mcsnet.ca or visit www.ideaman.net

Sales Success Secrets

Out of Sight – Out of Mind – Out of Business!

A long-term profitable sales career or business is built on acquiring and taking care of your clients. Many clients simply get ignored, forget who they bought their product or service from, or simply drift away. This can be devastating to your profit margins and survival.

To avoid this happening to you, please do this:

- Create a simple, yet systematic, process that will keep you in the top-of-mind position as a value-added resource to your clients.
- Remind them of their importance to you and your firm and learn ways to creatively touch base and market to them again and again.

What are you doing to help your valued clients remember you?

When I worked in the kitchen design field, I created little brass plaques that were installed, at eye level, on one of the more focal cabinets in the kitchen. Each 1' x 3' plaque had my client's name as well as mine and my company's. This generated interest, expressed professionalism, and helped with amazing referrals. If I were doing that today, it would have my website listed as well. I also had little stickers made with my name and design studio phone number and put them on some of the drawers.

In our speaking/training business (Ideas At Work! www.ideaman.net or www.BobHooey.training) we offer follow up e-zines, special offers, Thanksgiving cards, as well as Christmas cards, and a number of other means to keep in touch. We want to ensure that our clients don't forget us. We ensure that any piece of paper we share has our contact information included, so they can find us later. We've done that with www.successpublications.ca and www.PandemicPublishers.com too.

Client service is a critical foundation for continued relationship and increased long-term sales potential. Keep your clients satisfied and they will continue to purchase from you. It is a simple concept, but often missed by average companies and sales staff.

Point to Ponder: *"Obstacles are necessary for success because in Sales, as in all careers of importance, victory comes only after many struggles and countless defeats."* **Og Mandino**

Does it really make sense then that the clients with the smallest number of purchases in their baskets get the express lines?

Perhaps this is what led to the creation of on-line shopping and personal shopping services as increasingly viable and profitable alternatives.

- What are the frustrations facing your clients in dealing with you (or your competitors) and what specific remedies are you working to implement to offset them?
- How are you making dealing with you a more pleasant, hassle-free experience for your clients?
- How can you make you and your company easier to do business with for your clients?

Challenge: People have choices! With the explosion of internet-based business alternatives, people have more choices globally than ever before. This creates both challenges and opportunities for those of us who are sales professionals.

- What are you doing to ensure your availability and accessibility to your clients?
- How accessible are you?
- How have you harnessed the Internet to help you serve your clients better?
- Do you offer clients Internet based service or information alongside your personal or on-site attention?

Dear Mr. Hooey: Thank you for **elevating my Sales Team's knowledge** *during your sales management seminar in Tehran (Iran). I look forward to meeting you in person during your future seminars. Warm regards."* **Mendi Ghaemi, Managing Director, Bidar Group, Tehran, Iran**

Sales Success Secrets

Would You Buy from Yourself?

Conducting an image self-evaluation

"Perception is reality!" This is often the case in business dealings. People like to deal with people they like or trust. People base their business perceptions on the image we portray. That image is enhanced or blurred by how we act or present ourselves. This is especially true when looking at the factors that influence people to do business with us on a repeat basis. We may be able to 'sell' them once; but how do we ensure they continue wanting to deal with us?

Take a moment and give some honest feedback to yourself, based on your past 6 month's experience, in dealing with your customers. Look at this from both a personal perspective and from the perspective of the firm in which you apply your selling profession. Hint: The answers here might show you where you can improve your service, attract, and retain customers!

Point to Ponder: *"Few individuals during their lifetime come anywhere near exhausting the resources within them. There are deep wells of strength that are seldom used."* **Richard E. Boyd**

Discuss your answers (below) with your fellow selling professionals and your manager.

ASK YOURSELF:
- Is your image one of honesty and straightforward sincerity? How do you know?
- From the buyer's point of view, would you be considered reliable? Why is that true?
- Could you honestly say your customers received special benefits dealing with you not available from one of your competitors? What? Why?

- In their eyes, would you appear to be an expert in your field? Why would they say that?
- Have you been effective in helping solve their problems? How so?
- Would you say you handled complaints to their complete satisfaction? How? Share some examples.
- Is 'integrity' one of your watchwords? How does it show in your dealings?
- Other than your business dealings, would you think your customers believe you have their best interests and welfare at heart? Why?
- Do customers look at you as a good reliable source of product or service information? Why?
- Would the majority of your customers continue dealing with your business, even if a competitor offered slightly lower prices? Why would they do that?
- What percentage of your new customers come from referrals? Why is that number significant?
- How do you plan to keep yourself and your staff educated and current in your field?
- Describe how you keep in touch with past clients. Describe the results.

If you have been honest in your appraisal of your business operation you might have seen a few areas in which improvement would help.

Challenge: Go back over your answers and ask yourself:
- How can I improve how I service and seek my clients?
- How can I change what I offer them to more accurately reflect what they need?
- How can I make a difference in my career and my community by making the changes I see needed here?
- How can I equip my staff and co-workers to better reflect the changes needed?
- How can I partner with other business owners to strengthen and expand the way we do business and the services or products we deliver?
- How can you reorganize your business to allow you to enjoy your life better?

Honest reflection, followed by a commitment to act, will perform miracles. Time and time again, sales professionals have done some soul searching and come up with some great ways to re-invent their business and give their clients the long-term service they deserve!

The game of selling is best played with enthusiasm and openness. The successful sale professional is one who is always 'on-the-grow', and on the lookout for ways to do it better. Are you?

For your Sales Success Secrets library

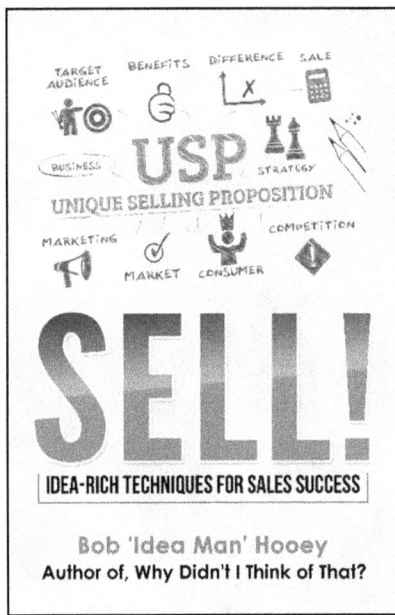

TARGET AUDIENCE BENEFITS DIFFERENCE SALE

BUSINESS **USP** STRATEGY
UNIQUE SELLING PROPOSITION

MARKETING MARKET CONSUMER COMPETITION

SELL!

IDEA-RICH TECHNIQUES FOR SALES SUCCESS

Bob 'Idea Man' Hooey
Author of, Why Didn't I Think of That?

"Sales can be a tough and sometimes complex, challenging, and confusing profession. It can also be fun!"

As a top performing professional salesperson, you need to identify individuals and organizations which you think may be interested in your product or service. You approach people who may or may not want to talk to you. When the opportunity to meet with a prospective client arises, you need to convince them that your product or service is better and/or more cost effective than your competitors!

Visit: www.amazon.com/SELL-Idea-rich-techniques-sales-success-ebook/dp/B07M68BRZD/ to get your own kindle copy.

Selling now days is done more online and less in person. Take advantage of these tips in how to effectively present in the new normal — on line. https://www.successpublications.ca/PIVOT.html

Sales Success Secrets

The Quality of Information You Receive Depends on the Quality of Your Questions
by Patricia Fripp

Patricia and I have been friends and colleagues for many years and even celebrate our birthdays on the same day. She is an expert in helping salespeople design and deliver their presentations for maximum impact.

As a seasoned sales professional, you are familiar with the importance of asking good questions in order to discover how a prospect can benefit from your product or service. The right questions give you good information that will move the conversation and process forward.

The Not-So-Basic Openers
The first priority is to learn as much as you can about pain points and about your prospect's current environment.
- What is your biggest challenge, and what do you think is the cause?
- How long has it been going on?
- Are you doing anything about it currently, or have you in the past?
- If you could solve it, what would that be worth?

Staying on Track
While you don't want to control the conversation too overtly, you need to focus on gaining an understanding of how they can benefit from a relationship with you. Use follow-up questions such as these for clarity:
- Can you give me a little more detail about that?
- Could you give me a specific example?
- How often does this happen?

Show Me the Money
Finding the decision-maker and/or economic buyer (the person who can sign the check) is paramount. If you are not sure, ask these questions:
- From whose budget would this investment come?
- Who can immediately approve this project or support this initiative?
- Can you help me better understand your purchasing process?

Point to Ponder: *"The real sale comes after the sale, reselling the customer you have to retain their business."* Patricia Fripp

Back-Pocket Questions
These are all-purpose but also particularly useful when you hear objections.
- Why do you say that about . . .?
- Can you help me better understand . . .?

Of course, the above questions are purposely generic to show the principles. Your questions will need to be tailored to your own circumstances. Consider this example from my own business. As a sales presentation skills coach and trainer, all my inquiries are incoming or referrals. I often hear, "What is your approach to sales presentation skills training?"

My goal is to ignore the question gracefully and find out more about them. I begin the conversation by finding where the inquiry came from. "Can we step backwards for a moment? Were you referred or am I the end of a web search?" Whatever the response, my next question is, "May I ask what just happened for you to be looking for a sales presentation skills trainer?" Quite often I hear, "We just lost a large sale we fully expected to win."

Now I go into mission mode, asking some of the following questions as they fit the circumstance:

- May I ask how much it would have been worth to your company if you had made the sale?
- Is that a small, medium, or large sale?
- How long is the life of a normal client?
- What is the average client worth to you?
- How many sales professionals do you have?
- How many final sales presentations do they deliver?
- Do you keep statistics on your closing rate?

Challenge: Can you see what I am finding out? 1) What the problem is; 2) how big the problem is; and 3) what it's costing the company. But here is the key: *You must let the prospect work out the cost for themselves.* Notice that at this point I have not told them how I will solve the problem.

Until you have the right information from the prospect, you do not know what approach to take to solve their problem. Remember, the prospect is more interested in themselves than in you. That means it is impossible to give a great presentation until you know where your focus needs to be.

© *Patricia Fripp www.fripp.com Used with permission*

Patricia Fripp, CSP, CPAE, Presentation Skills Expert, Creator of FrippVT Powerful Persuasive Presentations online learning system. In 2019, she was named one of the Top 25 Women in Sales.

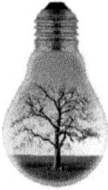

PRO-tips: honing your selling skills

- Sell solutions to challenges. Mediocre salespeople sell features; Average salespeople sell benefits; top performers sell solutions to perceived challenges.
- Leverage your selling time.
- Always be prospecting – always keep your pipeline full.
- Focus on quality – create quality conversations and pre-qualify.
- What is your next step? Schedule your next step or contact.
- Aim high! Start as high as you can in the organization and get referred down to the right decision maker.
- Be a boy scout… Always be prepared! Do your homework!
- Provide solid value. Buyers respect people who are experts in their trade who provide value.
- Understand your prospective client.
- Answer the why? E.g., why should I listen to you, why is your product or service better than the competition?

Sales Success Secrets

10 'Key' Strategies for Effective Sales and Business Presentations

Your **sales success** and/or business career depends on your ability to persuade an audience, employer, client, or buyer. These presentation tips will help you understand how to structure your sales presentation for maximum effect.

Challenge: These presentation tips can be used on your journey for both personal and professional success. Learn to apply them.

- **Keep it short:** Time is precious and more so as you move up the leadership chain. Value their time and keep it simple, short and to the point.
- **Know your audience:** Do your homework in advance so you can tailor or customize your presentation (sales, informative, product or service demonstration, interview) to your audience and get and keep their interest. This is critical in business and even more so in selling.
- **Use visuals to add interest:** Pictures, props, visuals help your audience capture and understand the point in a shorter period. Demonstrate to illustrate. (show and tell)
- **Get them involved:** Audience involvement and interaction is essential in this very competitive arena. If you have figures to be worked out, why not ask them to do so? (**Tip from a sales pro**: If it is their data, they trust it and give it more credibility.)
- **Start and end on time!** I can't emphasize this one enough. If you ask for 10-15 minutes of someone's time, you'd better be closing your mouth and your briefcase on or before the 10 or 15-minute mark. Or, on your closing slide. This is what separates the professionals from the mediocre performers. This works well in the world of professional speaking. As a professional speaker, I now ask my clients, "*When would you like me to finish my presentation?*" Often, I help them get back on schedule which they love.

- **Dress appropriately:** Dress for Success – not excess! Make a point of understanding the dress code for the specific client, group, or situation. One suggestion would be to always be a bit better dressed than the best dressed person in attendance. This helps to establish your credibility, more so in selling. If they don't buy you, they will not buy what you are selling.

- **Use short sentences and simple phrases:** Make it easy for the audience to gain acceptance and understanding of your concepts. Don't assume that they are fully literate – keep in mind most of the morning newspapers *(read by many executives)* are written to grade 6-8 levels.

- **Avoid humor unless relevant and appropriate:** Effective use of humor can be a great bridge to building bonds and relationships. However, you can blow yourself out of the running by using something that offends someone in the audience. They may not even tell you, but they won't buy from you or deal with you.

- **Distribute handouts or sales materials at end of your sales presentation:** This applies to any use of handouts, brochures, or other sales materials. Unless you need to have them refer to them, use them as a tool, or write something in them during your sales presentation – leave them for the end. People tend to read what you've given them instead of listening to you. Keep their focus on you!

- **Don't bluff. If you don't know, find out!** Your credibility is a *fragile* thing in the business arena. In selling, it is one of the crucial components to long-term success. When asked a question… be ready! Do your homework so you have the basics at your fingertips. You should never be surprised by a question. Don't try to wing it or fake it when asked a question outside that parameter. Or, if not… make sure you understand the question and make a specific commitment to find out and get back to them. Then do so!

Point to Ponder: *Business owners and leaders are busy, and you need to be clear and concise to win and keep their attention. Unless you know them, start strong, present value, and conclude with impact. Short and sweet gains their respect and often their business.*

Sales Success Secrets

Winning Attitudes Provide Foundations for Sales Success by Tim Breithaupt

Maintaining a positive attitude is a simple survival tool in the sales game. To be a top performing sales professional requires you to be able to endure a multitude of 'NOs' as well as the occasional negativity. Working to keep your attitude positive will pay off handsomely in your future.

In this chapter we, draw wisdom from proven sales master, friend, and best-selling author of **Take this Job and Love It, The Joys of Professional Selling, Tim Breithaupt.**

TIM: Attitude is the cornerstone of success. Top achievers understand the importance of a winning edge and are guided by positive attitudes of successful people who have gone before them. They hold themselves responsible for their quality of life. No excuses.

In sales, as in life, your attitude helps determine your altitude.

Choose success!

A growing body of research confirms that attitude has a compelling impact on success, empowering us to achieve new levels of productivity in our professional and personal lives. A positive approach can enrich our personality and enhance the impression we make on others.

In fact, a deeper appreciation of this may cause you to change your outlook and enthusiastically join those of us who consider a positive attitude to be our most priceless possession.

Here are my two definitions of attitude:
1) your outlook toward things
2) choice

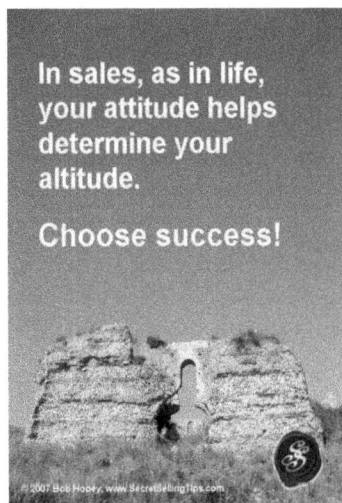

You are what you think. You can choose to be miserable today, or you can choose to make it a great day. My theory is that life is too short to be miserable, but it's long enough to have some fun.

Point to Ponder: *"Life offers choices; you can live a life of anticipation or a life of participation. The choice you make determines whether you live with results, or with excuses. You decide."* **Tim Breithaupt**

Unfortunately, as we navigate through a typical day we are bombarded with an onslaught of negative inputs. More than 75 per cent of what we hear, see, and read is negative.

Often, we succumb to these negative influences, living in quiet desperation under a tremendous burden of stress, failing to see the few slivers of positives around us.

The vaccine for this is to make a conscious choice to embrace and nurture a positive outlook. Seeing the positive is a discipline, it can be hard work. It takes conscious effort and energy to remain positive and energized throughout the day.

Consider this... For every mile of road to success there are two miles of ditch'

Another saboteur of positive attitudes is a lack of daily goals. I call them *'daily destinations'.* We often go into our day guided by nothing more than a sense of routine and familiar habit, our daily outcomes determined by the urgency of other people's objectives. Without goals or destinations of our own, we inevitably become subservient to the demands of others. The sad fact is that up to 80 per cent of our day can be re-active versus pro-active.

You can offset this silent theft of time if you are guided by clearly defined *'daily destinations'.* Know where your finish line is for each and every day. Experience the euphoria of a productive day versus a day of mere busyness. This simple yet effective strategy will put more enjoyment in your life, one day at a time.

'Chase two rabbits and both will escape.' Tim Breithaupt

Start today by planning your tomorrows. Fulfill your daily commitments fueled by a sense of optimism – guided by clarity of purpose. **Make it a great day.**

Challenge: Ask your sales manager, your close and trusted friends, or a sales colleague you respect, to evaluate your attitude and give you their honest feedback. Then act on it as needed.

- Are you *generally* a positive person? How does that reveal itself? Ask for examples.
- How positive is your language? Remember, what you talk about, you bring about.
- How do you handle the *occasional* setbacks, detours, or bumps in your sales path to success? Do you learn from them and move on, or do you get bogged down?

Choose success in maintaining a positive attitude and daily acting from that perspective.

For more articles from Tim and other sales experts visit: www.SuccessPublications.ca/SalesArticles.htm

"Bob; The **structure that your materials** *(Secret Selling Tips)* **have supplied us has been priceless.** *The consistent automated communication keeps us on track learning and growing as a sales driven company. For the* **small investment** *we have seen individuals hitting goals that they thought in the past were untouchable."* **Fred Schweinert, Steinhafel's Furniture, Wisconsin**

How to Up Sell for Increased Sales and Commissions

One of the secrets to your success as a sales professional is effectively handling up sales. It is one thing to get the sale, it is better to *'biggie-size'* that sale. Often for you and the client/customer this is the best deal! It is a more profitable use of your time, for sure.

As a sales professional – remember you are there to *'help'* your clients.

Up Selling is easier when you consider your main business as *'sincerely'* helping your clients.

Being a 'trusted advisor' is the key.

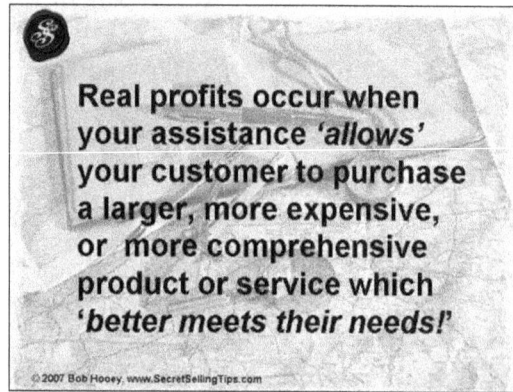

Real profits occur when your assistance *'allows'* your customer to purchase a larger, more expensive, or more comprehensive product or service which *'better meets their needs!'*

© 2007 Bob Hooey, www.SecretSellingTips.com

Think about the problems your clients/customers encounter. What does it REALLY take to assist them and to solve their problems? That's your job!

Chances are your client needs *'substantially'* more than the simple inexpensive solution or purchase they first consider when approached. By grouping together several different products and services, you can give the client a more comprehensive, relevant, or advanced package that goes much further toward creating a long-term satisfying solution.

Sometimes you need to suggest a *'superior'* version of a product that will fit the needs or has the capacity *to grow* with their changing needs. It might be more expensive now, but it will be cost effective in the long run. The foundation for this approach is laid when you invest time finding out their needs and concerns, prior to showing them specific products. They will thank you for being a true sales professional and not just selling them what they ask for; but helping them purchase what they need and what will best suit those needs over the long haul.

Point to Ponder: *"There are risks and costs to any program of action. But they are far less that the long-range risks and costs of comfortable inaction."* **John F. Kennedy**

Two simple ways to make Up Selling automatic and easy for the client

Here are two field proven ways to build up selling into any purchase. Use these and clients/customers will often buy two or three times as much without giving it much thought. Many sales professionals have seen their sales double and triple simply by incorporating these techniques into their normal sales process and conversations.

Bundle, design, group, or package several related or complementary products or services together. Drop the price below what the total would be if the customer bought all the products individually.

When a prospective client inquires about a single item, investigate what they need and then educate him or her that they can get that item, PLUS a great deal more by purchasing your bundle, design group, or special package. Make sure you leverage off this design advantage for additional sales.

You will find many prospective clients just can't resist the bundle, design group, or package deal bargain. Announce your new bundle, design group, or package deal with flair.

It works fine by itself, but it REALLY works when you add THIS.

If your product or service works much better with a complimentary or plug-in item, be sure to tell your prospective clients about it. That is good salesmanship.

It is surprising how many products and services fit hand in glove. It's hard to have one without needing the other. If it makes their job easier or meets their unspoken needs, you are acting as a true sales professional in offering them a series of options. Electronic Sales professionals know to ask if you need extra cables, connections, or companion pieces to allow your central purchase to work to your benefit. This can work as well in the furniture areas with the addition of accessories, rugs, lighting, etc. It also works in many other fields and industries.

Successful up selling needs to be at the core of every business or professional practice. It can *instantly* multiply your production, commissions, and profits. You might well go from just getting by to living comfortably and from living comfortably to rolling in wealth from happy customers earning you larger commissions.

Challenge: How familiar are you with your opportunities to assist your customers by up selling them? Ask your senior consultants for help to enhance your expertise.

If you are sales professional and committed to helping your customers get what they need, you will create the opportunity to demonstrate that commitment on a regular basis. People will respond and reward you with additional orders. They will remember you and refer you to others who can use your products or services. That's a triple win in my books.

Customer service is a success tool for the top performing professional, business owner, and champion salesperson. It amazes them when you call – so few salespeople do!

It helps convert them into your champions and fans, when you follow-up and ensure they are happy. When you find out early when something is not working correctly or needs adjustment, fix it! Have you worked to make it easier for your clients to find you, get the information they need, and track their order or service process? UPS and FEDEX use on-line tracking systems, which is really a very effective sales and marketing tool.

Michael Hammer drives home the point about being **ETDBW** (easy to do business with) in *'The Agenda'*. Add it to your sales library! How easy are you to do business with?

How Well Do You Know Or 'Profile' Your 'Ideal' Client/Customer?

Do you have a profile built for your typical or target client/customer? What is it? How big is your potential market? For example: in Canada, 33 billion is spent yearly on furniture, home furnishings, and appliances. The US the figure is likely 10 to 15 times higher. **How much of that would you like to capture?**

Do you have market segments you serve that have different profiles? For example, in the area of home furnishings 84% of the buying decisions are made by women. How does information like that impact what you are doing and how you approach your potential customers?

One of our national clients has recently re-defined the 3 major markets which make up 38% of the Canadian population.

> Qualifying can be much easier when you have a better idea or model of your ideal or target customer in mind

© 2007 Bob Hooey, www.SecretSellingTips.com

For example: their primary customer is a female home provider (aged 39-45); their secondary customer is a female 'baby-boomer'; while their third is the emerging young adult market. They have invested in this research as well as the training of their sales teams across the country in recognizing and serving them more effectively.

Point to Ponder: *"The world of tomorrow belongs to the person who has the vision today."* **Robert Schuller**

Ask yourself:
Who is your ideal client/customer? What do you know about their needs, desires, wants, work, income level, etc.?

- What motivates them to make purchases in your industry?
- What has changed in their world, industry, or roles that may have impacted how they shop, make choices, or evaluate purchases or decisions?
- Have you created probing questions that, when answered, will help you better serve these ideal customers?

So, who is your 'ideal' client/customer? Who would you love to do business with on an ongoing basis? Who would you love to be working with now or in the long-term?

- Is it someone who is able to see the value in what you offer?
- Is it someone who has an obvious, demonstrated need for your service or products?
- Is it someone who has the ability and the capacity to afford what you offer? Who can actually buy what you sell?
- Is it someone who will purchase repeatedly from you?
- Is it someone who pays his or her bills on time and is a low maintenance, or non-demanding customer? (Oh, yes!)
- Is it someone who willingly refers you to other qualified prospects and becomes a champion or center of influence on your behalf? (Amen)

Sounds like a *dream* customer, doesn't it? In reality, there are people out there who will match this, or other criteria in your search to build your sales career. The *secret* is establishing some criteria to help you recognize them or at least recognize those who don't match up. Essentially when you define and state your needs you start *attracting* these people. In addition, you start *noticing* them quicker when they visit your store.

Low performing sales staff often neglect investing sufficient time in the pre-qualifying process. Sales professionals who are consistently top earners know *exactly* who they should be looking for and dealing with to be successful. Taking time to ensure your prospect '*actually*' qualifies can make your sales career more than successful – it can transform it into a superstar launching pad.

Challenge: During your next down time, when you have a minute; go through the above exercise and define or visualize your ideal customer within your market.

If you want to be productive, make a tremendously outrageous income, still have a life, and be able to enjoy the fruits of your labour -- this might be a good exercise for you. Invest some time exploring who you would like to have as a long-term customer. Interestingly enough, this works very well. ☺

For your Sales Success Secrets library

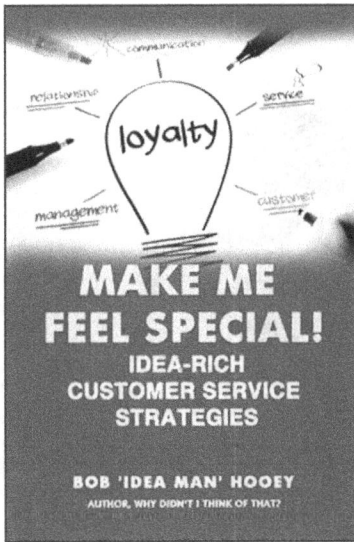

Business success, whether retail, service-based, or even direct buyer connection, is built by establishing mutually profitable relationships: relationships where you make the customer (client) feel special. When you 'Make ME Feel Special!' you enhance your chances to convert me from a one-time customer to a raving fan and long-term profitable client and avid champion. You 'make money' in business when you are in face-to-face or phone-to-phone sales, service, or follow up contact with your clients. You 'earn that money' by delivering on what you contract and you 'leverage that money' by maintaining good client contact and superior service.

But first, you need to be and/or keep in contact with them. Keep in touch, treat them special, and they will come back; and bring their friends and colleagues too.

Visit: www.amazon.com/Make-Feel-Special-Idea-rich-strategies/dp/1790300924/ to get your personal copy.

Dealing with PRICE Objections

One of the biggest challenges faced by many in the sales field is how to *effectively* counter these 5 words **'Your Price is TOO High!'** Customers have learned to leverage this phrase to get what *'they'* want, a better price. All too often, less professional sales staff cave and start carving the heart out of their commissions and their company's margins in pursuit of the deal. This is counterproductive and not in anyone's best interest.

Investing time understanding and effectively countering objections will pave the way for increased sales and higher commissions. It will also help you reduce the stress of dealing with this *paper tiger* in your day-to-day customer relationships. It will help your company be more profitable too.

Ever find yourself dealing with a situation or competitor where price becomes an issue? I'd suggest buying a good sales book and boning up on the basic sales techniques, but here are a few ideas that might jog your mind in preparation.

In the case of a *commodity*-based perception, price is the primary key. Moving away from being perceived in that commodity category is a value-based activity. Getting your clients to see the value makes their financial decision easier.

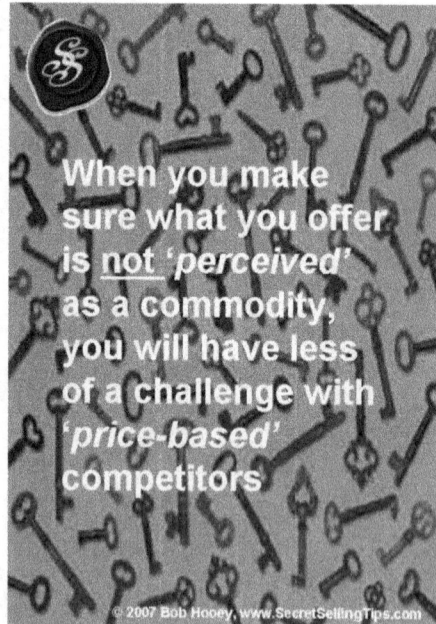

When you make sure what you offer is not *'perceived'* as a commodity, you will have less of a challenge with *'price-based'* competitors

© 2007 Bob Hooey, www.SecretSellingTips.com

Here are a number of proven tips for handling objections when they come up, and they will.

- **Separate your ego from the sale** – it is not about you – it is about helping them.
- **Build a 'possible objections' file** and be able to answer them honestly.
- **Positive anticipation of objections** – deal with objections in your presentation
- **Assist the client in saving face** – sometimes they really can't buy from you.
- **Listen with ALL your senses** – look and listen to draw them out.
- **Persistence pays off** – don't back off simply because they raise an objection. The true professional knows he or she may have to negotiate a number of no's to get to the yes.

Three-step objections model

- **Clarify** – let me see if I understand this…
- **Buffer** – share some information that buffers the objection
- **Answer** their objection with a return to *benefit*-based statements.

Point to Ponder: "Remember, you only have to succeed the last time." Brian Tracy

Answering PRICE objections using some of these tried-and-true sales techniques. Here is where you dig into your sales library to learn how each of these techniques work. One or several of them might be effective in a Sales situation. Having more tools allows you to be more productive and valuable to potential clients.

Here they are:

- Use the subtraction method.
- Don't be afraid to cast doubt.
- Reinforce the quality.
- Ask hypothetical questions.
- Go for the trial close.
- Draw buyer's attention away from price.
- Sell and build loyalty.
- Share success stories.

- Risk of 'cheapness'.
- Work on buying dissonance.
- Reverse tactic.
- Alternate-advantage overload.
- Competition to meet standards.
- Future order.
- Bottom line response.

Three most common price objections – and how to counter them.
Professionals in the sales business have taken the time to look at their products or services and to become knowledgeable in answering questions concerning each of the benefits, features, policies, and procedures.

Similarly, they have taken the time to think through their response to the following very basic objections:
- **I don't have the money** (budget)
- **I can buy it cheaper somewhere else** (really – same product vs. similar?)
- **I don't see your value in this**...

Challenge: How would you respond when a prospect uses one of these objections?

Your answer may just be the secret to your ongoing success in this field of sales. These common objections should never be a *surprise* to the sales professional. **Be ready to sell!**

PRO-tip: Know your sales cycle
Different businesses have different sale cycles, which is the time from initial contact to closing the deal. Check your last 20 closed deals to see how long they took and work out your average.

Then work to enhance and improve it during the remainder of this year.

Sales Success Secrets

Proactive Strategies to Minimize Price Objections

More on dealing with price challenges. How do you compete when you know you aren't the least expensive in your area or industry?

How do you compete in an increasingly competitive global market?

Here are a few areas that will help in this regard.

Conduct a Strategic Value Analysis
Taking the time to find out a bit about these four areas will help you build a strong foundation and relationship to better service your customers. Better relationships will take the pressure of the price factor in the buying decision. The more you know, the better you can apply that knowledge in serving those who need what you provide.

- **Market Analysis**
- **Competitive Analysis**
- **Self-analysis**
- **Customer analysis**

Positioning Strategies – to create barriers
The more successful companies have carved out a position as the quality leader in their field. This emphasis on quality or value moves the evaluation process away from price.

Outsmart the competition
Use your brains and look for ways to better service your customers. Find ways to provide services or value-added products that your competition doesn't.

Leverage all your resources

Being lean and mean in using your resources helps you to keep your overhead in line and keep your pricing competitive. Leveraging your resources fully allows you to better serve as well.

Decide on all organizational needs

Invest the time to streamline your operation and its processes. Keep it simple! This will help your staff provide the best service possible. It also allows your customers to see firsthand your commitment to giving them value for their dollar. Think repeat business!

Work to generate end-user support

If you are in the position of being a supplier – your customers are really your 'customers' customers (end users). How can you help your customers by working to reach and teach the end users? Become a drawing point or success partner for your clients/customers.

Challenge: Value-added Checklist (10 minimum – go for 20)

Bundling

How about making what you offer more valuable by combining products or services to allow your customers lots of options. What types of bundles can you offer? Take a moment and brainstorm.

Proactive probing

Invest the time to find out what moves your customers. What keeps them up at night? Ask questions and respond to what you learn, by adapting or changing your business. This is one way of keeping what you offer current, valuable, and viable.

Point to Ponder: *"The individual (the customer) perceives service in his or her own terms."* Arch McGill

Reinforce value

Everything you do should be focused on reinforcing the value in what you offer. What is the true value of what you offer? Warranty, service, selection, delivery, options?

Sell intangibles

Often the true value of what you sell is based on things that can't be shown or proven until needed, as above. Do you have a better warranty? Do you offer better terms? Do you offer a better selection or stocking? Do you offer expert advice or consulting? Do you offer delivery and installation? **Let them know!**

Don't be shy about sharing your unique value proposition. If you are shy – you'll die in a competitive market.

Presentation ideas

When you get an opportunity to present or share about your business or products – I'd suggest looking for ways to incorporate the following areas into your sales process. You can be a great spokesman if you do. This will also be a tremendous assist in helping them decide to deal with you – closing can be a challenge. But these hints will help you be more effective in signing up additional business and retaining clients.

How can you...?

- Demonstrate earnings
- Cut their costs
- Go for agreement to product first
- Carefully choose your words
- Use proper sales terms instead of jargon
- Sandwich the price - focus on value (good, better, best!)
- Price with benefits summary
- Cost as a 'mere' fraction
- Minimize the cost-to-own
- Analogize – not apologize
- Use relevant testimonials wherever possible
- Think and talk 'long-term'
- Present deal in its best light

These critical impact areas are essential to being a value-based, sales and customer service business. Look for ways to build them into your business. The effort you invest will pay off – BIG TIME, and long-term!

Sales Success Secrets

What Is Your Closing Ratio?

'What is your closing ratio?' That's a critical question for each selling professional to ask themselves. The majority of salespeople I've talked to, say they don't know. And the *'rare'* salesperson who does answer, gives me something vague like:

- **My closing ratios are 20 percent**
- **My closing ratios are 45 percent**
- **I close 80 percent of all my opportunities**

I might ask a follow up question, 'What kind of statistical records do you keep?' Often their answer is they don't keep any detailed records. Hmmmm! A further challenging question, 'So how do you *really* know what your closing ratio is?'

I often experience a **'long, sometimes painful silence'** as they reflect on the answer to that question. How would you respond?

I am amazed at how few in the selling professionals record and revisit their numbers to see how they are doing and where they can improve. We might know how much we sold (sales totals) made or generated in commissions; but when asked, would be hard pressed to provide analytical data to demonstrate how well we did in our efforts.

- How about you?
- Do you want to sell more?
- Do you want to know if your hard work and selling effort is getting results?

If so, you need to set up and keep detailed records.

HINT: When you maintain more detailed and accurate records and act on that information, you'll be equipped to close more sales, in less time, and with less effort. Works for me.

A quick look at closing ratios

There are a variety of methods or ways you can look at closing ratios. In the most general sense, each time you engage or create a sales opportunity (where you think someone is going to buy something from you) you record it as an opportunity in a spreadsheet or simple table.

If that person did, in fact, engage your services or purchase from you, you closed the sale. Seems simple, doesn't it? Record your results over specific periods of time, and you have your closing ratio.

If that is too general or broad, you might track the number of proposals you make and deliver to a prospect. Keep track of the number of people who engage your services or purchase and again, you have your closing ratio. But closing ratios shouldn't be the only determining factor.

Consider these criteria:
- Number of times you actually meet with the client/customer before you close the sale.
- Length of time it takes to close the sale.
- Average amount of the sale.

Your numbers and results are impacted, in part, by the sales cycle which differs for each client and industry. For example, if you are selling complex or big-ticket items your sales cycle might run up to a year. If you are in retail, it might be a matter of 10 minutes or a few days.

Number of meetings with customer prior to close
You may not have realized this secret, but selling is, in essence, a time management issue.

Challenge: It's critical to know how many times you must meet with a client/customer before he/she buys from you. What percentage of your sales close on the first interview? The second? The third? The fifth? The twentieth?

Why is this important? Because if you've got to have multiple meetings with the customer, you're probably wasting a lot of time and getting very little in the way of results.

I've worked with a variety of selling professionals who sell retail as well as consulting services, tax services, design services, financial services, software, insurance, and so on. In most instances, we get a sense that a sale will be made in either the first or second meeting: *'if'* we are dealing with (qualified) demonstrated pain or need, talking to a decision-maker, and there is, at least, an appearance of an ROI (return on investment) for the potential customer. (The keys we all learned about sales.)

Despite this, many of those same selling professionals were spending 40-50 percent or more of their time doing third, fourth, or more, calls. These calls seldom close, are less profitable, and clearly drive down revenue, yet they continued to make them.

I've learned is to draw a line in the sand. By that I mean, know when to say enough, say good-bye or move on to someone who is going to buy now. I've challenged salespeople to define their ideal client, learn how to clearly communicate what they do, and invest time to create materials and sales tools that will answer questions and limit the perception of risk for their potential clients/customers.

If the potential customer doesn't buy or commit to a buying process (plan) by the end of call two, and they do actually fit your target profile, don't just throw them away or forget about them.

My suggestion: Set them up as part of a communications process that helps them get more familiar and educated about you and that they can feel safe deciding.

Several ideas:
- Regular email or -e-letters
- Post cards or calls about new products and services being introduced

- Mail out product information or emails with links to information they might be interested in learning.

This simple approach frees up a huge portion of your time and will allow you to spend more time networking, looking for new clients, and delivering value to their target market. It would also help you make more money too.

Point to Ponder: *"For every sale you miss because you're too enthusiastic, you will miss a hundred because you're not enthusiastic enough."* Zig Ziglar

Sales cycle

A second *critical* factor (mentioned earlier) is the length of your sales cycle. That is, how long does it *normally* take, from the day (time) you engage or create a sales opportunity, to the day you have a signed order or actually ring up the sale?

When you know what that length of time is, your challenge as a selling professional is to discover practical, innovative ways to shorten it.

My experience with salespeople teaches me that most spend too much time telling the prospect all about their:
- Wonderful or great products or services.
- Their years of experience in the business or their industry.
- The large number of customers their company does business with.

Frankly, your typical customer does not care about any of these unless they apply to their specific needs.

What they fail to do is ask great questions, so they can discover what it is that the customer is trying to accomplish. **Gee, that sounds like qualifying again.**

When the salesperson doesn't clearly understand the customer's issues (goals and objectives, problems, special challenges), they are unable to make a strong case that what they are offering is a viable and mutually profitable solution. (qualifying) For that reason, the decision is often delayed or put off until later. Meanwhile, the salesperson calls every few weeks asking, 'Do you want to move ahead with (insert product or service)?' Wonder if you've ever been in that position?

Here's something to consider: If a customer really has a problem or need, why wouldn't she want to do something about it? Today?

In retail this might not be as obvious, as our customers simply leave, shop, and very often buy from someone else. Whether you are in retail or making site calls a part of your selling process, asking great questions will help you close more business.

For example, in dealing with a corporate client you might want to ask questions that determine:
1) what the prospect company was really trying to accomplish,
2) what the daily, weekly, and monthly cost of delay was,
3) what the ROI was on buying.

Understanding the principles behind these questions will help you succeed in any industry.

What do you earn on each sale?
The amount of money you earn on each sale is important. If your average earnings on each sale are in the thousands of dollars, you can afford to invest more time in the opportunity than if you're only making a couple of hundred dollars.

For example, a real estate broker could earn $10,000, $25,000 or $100,000, on a single transaction. A mortgage broker could be earning $1000, $2000, or $5000 per transaction. Someone selling insurance may make no more than $300, $500 or $1000 on a single sale.

If you've got to meet with someone two, three or four times to close the sale and you're only going to make $150 in commissions you're not making much money, especially when you factor in travel, expenses, preparation, and other time.

Separate buyers from non-buyers. When you know what your closing ratios are, you might need to improve your skills so you can do a better job of separating buyers and non-buyers, in the shortest time.

If your prospect isn't going to buy, you're better off knowing it sooner, rather than later. You don't want to follow up with a prospect for 30, 60 or 90 days and then discover you aren't going to make a sale.

When a salesperson tells me their closing ratio is 20 percent, they're really saying that **80 percent of their time is being wasted.** If they only wasted 50 percent of their time, their business would double.

Challenge: Think about this...

- When you close your opportunities, you sell 100 percent of those who are going to buy.
- When you don't close your opportunities, you fail to sell 100 percent of those who are *not* going to buy.

Your real problem may not be in your closing ratios, but in your inability to identify who is, or is not, a prospect. (Qualifying)

Bonus tips: Five ways to grow your business.

Here are five strategies you can use to dramatically improve your business:

1. **Find more prospects.** Spend more time looking for people who need your products or services.

2. **Look for new people.** Get out of your comfort zone. Call on people you've never spoken with before.

3. **Ask better questions. (Pre-qualify)** Spend more time searching for the issues that are important to the customer instead of telling her all about yourself, your company, and your products.

4. **Use the telephone more.** The telephone is a great time-saver. Spend more time calling prospects and use the phone to pre-qualify them before you have a face-to-face meeting.

5. **Prune your database.** Remove bad prospects from your database. Stop calling on people that you've called on forever and who have not done business with you.

Sales Success Secrets

Closing... When and Where?

Over the years we shared closing techniques with our Secret Selling Tips subscribers. Properly used, these techniques help you bring your sales conversations to a 'yes' that begins building a long term, mutually profitable relationship. (*Included in this book*)

I get newer or less professional salespeople who ask me "When they should unleash or use these 'trick' closes?" My answer is "...never, unless you want to remain an ineffective, underperforming salesperson and eventually find another job."

Now some of you would say, **"Bob, I thought these 'trick' closes would help me sell more."** You would be correct, **for the short term!** My intent here is to challenge you to grow and to expand your sales toolbox in your quest to be a better, more profitable, sales professional.

As in many areas, it is your *'intent'* or *'motivation'* in employing any close, 'trick' or otherwise that can make them destructive and have them backfire in what you want, an ongoing, profitable relationship. **'Trick' closes tend to hurt your credibility by creating a high-pressure sales environment.** This seldom works with more informed clients and can actually create an offense as they see through obviously manipulative closes. Be very careful how you close, but don't be afraid to do so!

These 'trick' or obvious closes actually tend to be sales blockers or sales killers when your clients figure out you are employing them against them. **People love to buy – they just don't like being sold!**

Here are a few obvious ones to avoid:

Puppy-dog close: In this very well-known close the salesperson offers the client a 'no-obligation' or free trial, following which the product can be returned. In this instance, you are gambling that your client will enjoy, become attached to it, or forget to return it by the agreed time, resulting in a sale. Check your motivation.

However: This can be an effective close when a trial is appropriate to allow your client to check it out and to be comfortable with their purchase. Don't be afraid to offer it if it really helps the client.

Reverse close: In this technique the salesperson asks a question looking for a 'no' answer which is really a 'yes' response. For example, "Is there any reason, if we could provide this (product or service) at this price, that you wouldn't do business with us?" This really doesn't work and can backfire if the client feels manipulated.

Assumptive close: This has been overdone to death. In this close, the salesperson asks a question which, if the client answers, *supposedly commits* them to a course of action. For example, "Would you like that in red or blue?" or, "Would delivery be better on Tues or Friday?"

Fly fishing or limited time offer close: In this technique the salesperson promises the prospective client a special discount (say 10-15% off). However, the discount is only valid if they order today. Now this can be effective in helping some cautious clients to make a move if it is real. More sophisticated clients can turn this against you. However: This close is fine **if it is *not* being employed as a pressure tactic** to get them to purchase quickly.

I can remember having to ask for assistance from my fellow kitchen design sales staff when I called a few clients to remind them of a special offer for free countertops that was 'actually' running out that evening. In this case, it was a legitimate offer from our factory for orders they received by the end of that day (Midnight BC). Eight of them came in during the day to take advantage of this very generous offer and I had to ask for help in processing their orders before the deadline.

Am I saying don't use any of these closes or the others we've shared with you? Of course not! **What I am saying is be very clear in your intent or motivation** to help the client make the best purchase or deal, for them. Make sure your focus is on being the best-selling professional they have ever met and one who is dedicated on genuinely helping them. Then, selectively use your professional sales tools in helping build a long term, mutually profitable relationship.

For your Sales Success Secrets library

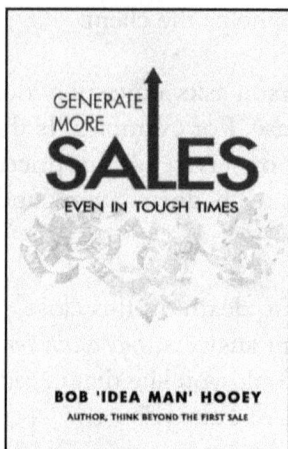

GENERATE MORE
SALES
EVEN IN TOUGH TIMES

BOB 'IDEA MAN' HOOEY
AUTHOR, THINK BEYOND THE FIRST SALE

How to gain the winning edge on your competition, 'even' in tough times. We have encountered 'tough times' in the past and are currently working through another series of challenges on a global level. Many salespeople are 'ASK' resistant – they are afraid to ask for the sale. As a result, they fail to meet or exceed their full potential in the sales arena." Sales can be a challenging arena, 'even' more so in tough times. I believe these little tips as laid out in this book can help you generate more sales, and repeat business, in spite of your circumstances. **They work, if you do!**

www.amazon.com/Generate-More-Sales-tough-times/dp/1530916372/

Bonus tips: From experience there are three basic referrals...

1) **Solicited:** Here you would simply ask for and hopefully receive a referral from a current or existing client.
2) **Proactive:** Without prompting or a request from you an existing client calls to give you the name of someone they think would be interested in what you have to offer.
3) **Unsolicited:** This is where your clients become your fans and champions in marketing you based on their experience and increased trust in what you offer.

A quick note about soliciting referrals at the point of sale. Many salespeople ask for the referrals at the time of the sale This can be awkward for the client and may even cause them to change their mind. Why? In truth, at this point they are taking a risk in placing the order or purchasing from you. You haven't earned their trust yet, so why would you want to ask and increase the pressure they are experiencing?

Wouldn't it be more effective to wait awhile until you have delivered on your promises and demonstrated your commitment to knock their socks off service and then ask?

Reasons People Buy and Keep On Buying

Knowing *'why'* people make purchases will allow you to position and continually re-position yourself and your company to help them do so. This insight will also give you an edge to retaining them as long-term clients and repeat buyers. You increase your ability to serve and sell your customers when you make the effort to view your products and services *through* their eyes.

Geoff Ayling, in his excellent book, **Rapid Response Advertising**, outlines fifty reasons why people buy.

Understand why your customers buy...

Then appeal to those emotions

© 2007 Bob Hooey
www.SecretSellingTips.com

There may be more than 50, but our guess is these 25 will get your creative sales juices flowing.

I'd suggest using these top 25 emotional reasons why people buy and keep on buying, 'even' in tough times.

To make money

To save money

To save time

To avoid effort

To gain comfort

To improve health

To escape pain

To be popular

To attract the opposite sex

To gain praise

To conserve our possessions

To increase our enjoyment

To satisfy curiosity

To protect our family

To protect our family

To be in style

To satisfy an appetite

To emulate others

To have beautiful things

To avoid criticism

To avoid trouble

To take advantage of opportunities

To be individual and unique

To protect our reputation.

To gain control over specific aspects of our lives

To be or feel safe

Whether you are talking one-on-one, presenting to a group of people, or communicating in writing, your audience, team, or readers will be evaluating and reacting to your words and 'filtering' them through one or more of the above emotional needs.

Point to Ponder: *Thomas Jefferson said, "The art of life is the art of avoiding pain; and he is the best pilot, who steers clearest of the rocks and shoals with which it is beset."*

Tough sell; isn't it? But if you have done your homework, and know a little bit about the needs, background and thought processes of those you want to reach, it will be much easier. You can enhance your chances of success by carefully crafting your communication to touch or draw on the emotional needs of your audience, team, or readership. But be cautious in its use.

Some would ask, isn't this manipulation? My gut reaction would be to say no! On the surface it might appear that way, but only you know your 'true' motives.

If your 'true' motive is to communicate more clearly, more effectively, and your desire is to serve them by giving them all the information they need in a way that makes it easier for them to relate to it – then I say go for it! Having an honest desire to help people is what builds a solid foundation for success under your career or business and helps ensure both longevity and success.

So, remember that communication, especially effective communication, is really a process of selling – selling your ideas, your desires, your dreams, and your future.

How effective will you be in persuading people to buy in? How successful will you be in inspiring them to help you? It's up to you!

Challenge: Go through this emotional buying list with an eye to the products and services you offer your clients. How can you better position them to leverage this buying emotion?

See how many of these top 25 buying reasons already fit with your product and service offerings. Discuss how you might adapt, amend, or add on to what you currently offer to make yourself more a more attractive resource for meeting your customer's needs over a longer time.

This is one of the selling secrets of getting repeat business – give your client a series of *valid* emotional reasons to do so!

Only 1 In 7 Sellers Do This Critical Skill
by Jill Konrath

I never wanted to be in sales. I only entered the profession because I had an idea for a business. When I shared it with a consultant, he said it was a good plan and timely. Then he asked, "Who's going to be doing the sales?" I was disgusted by the question. Ugh. I shuddered, then leaned forward and said in a most accusing manner, "I thought you said it was a good idea."

He replied, "It is, Jill. **But somebody has to sell it**." After thinking about it, I begrudgingly entered the sales profession to learn what I needed to do to sell my idea, getting myself hired by Xerox.

I gave myself ONE YEAR to learn everything I needed to know ... which meant I was a total sponge, a student, someone who was hell-bent on mastering this profession as quickly as I could.

That meant I studied everything – even my own performance. I had to figure out what worked and what didn't, what approaches were most effective, and which caused problems. I enjoyed considerable success, fairly fast and actually started to enjoy selling.

Fast-forward a few years ... I was still at Xerox and had been selected to attend a Management Development workshop in Washington DC for high performing sellers with leadership potential.

That's when I heard the statistic.
Sitting in class, I was stunned when the instructor said, "Only one in seven salespeople self-assess after a sales meeting." *How could that be?* I instantly thought. To me, it was a standard operating procedure. I assumed everyone did it. All the time. Then, the instructor added, "…. and those who do are the top performers."

Bingo! It made total sense to me. After all, how could you get any better if you didn't analyze your own performance on a regular basis.

Yet over 85% of sellers didn't do it. Maybe they didn't know how.

Maybe they didn't want to be at fault. Maybe they didn't even know why it made a difference. But it did. It mattered tremendously.

If a person didn't self-assess, they'd be stuck in mediocrity, blissfully unaware that top performers were doing anything differently from them. Or, they'd get progressively discouraged, questioning if they were cut out for sales and ultimately quitting, leaving me to fill an open territory.

Hearing this statistic was a defining moment for me. It reaffirmed my own behaviors. I'd unwittingly stumbled into a best practice because of my impatience to learn sales and leave the profession.

As an emerging sales leader, I realized that I'd never be successful unless I could teach my salespeople how to think about what their actions and strategies in a way that enabled them to continuously improve.

Over time, I realized that questions were my best tool in helping salespeople get better. They provoked curiosity and implied that there were alternative ways to do things. (I've listed some helpful ones here.) The ensuing discussions led to lots of impromptu role-plays, where sellers could test out new ways of doing things. It was all an experiment in getting better.

I loved exploring my salespeople's challenges (aka issues, obstacles, objections, delays, losses) the most. My goal was to help each person get to the root cause of their particular selling problem.

For example, it was a great learning opportunity – or example, when a prospect asked about price early on in the meeting – and upon learning it quickly replied, "We don't have any money in the budget." "Mmmm," I'd say to my salesperson, "Based on my experience, something you said elicited that response. What were you talking about just before your prospect brought up the budget issue?"

Then we'd backtrack, review their actions, brainstorm different approaches, and do quick mock meetings to see if they could possibly lead to better responses. It got salespeople thinking. Exploring. Testing.

Assuming personal responsibility for their success. Getting better. By showing my reps how to self-assess on a regular basis, their sales results improved enabling them to outperform even their own expectations.

While that "1 in 7" statistic has haunted me my entire career, I am eternally grateful I learned it early on. It's a difference maker!

Challenge: Self-Assessment Questions
Here are some good questions you can ask yourself or your reps. Use them after a phone call or a sales meeting.

Overall
- How do you think that call/meeting went?
- Did you accomplish your objective?
- If not, was it a realistic one?
- Is the next meeting on the calendar? If not, what happened?

What Went Well
- As you review the call/meeting, what were the best parts?
- What were you doing then that was so effective?
- How can you integrate that into future conversations?

What Needed Improvement
- What surprised you, put you off your game?
- What did you forget to do/say/ask that could make a difference?
- Where did you run into trouble? What do you think caused that?
- What could you have done things differently? What else? What else?
- To get the maximum impact, use these questions frequently. Make them a regular part of your personal self-assessment or your sales management process.

© **Jill Konrath www.jillkonrath.com Used with permission.** *Jill's sales career has been defined by her relentless search for fresh strategies that actually work in an ever-changing business environment. She's the bestselling author of four books: Selling to Big Companies, SNAP Selling, Agile Selling, and More Sales Less Time. 2019 LinkedIn named Jill as their #1 Business-to-Business Sales Expert. Salesforce selected her as one of Top 7 Sales Influencers of the 21st century. Plus, she's a featured expert in the brand new "Story of Sales" documentary.*

The Seven 'Be-Attitudes' of Good Service

Customer Service is one of the foundations for any enduring success in sales or business. Customer Service depends on more than just a *'catchy slogan'* to engage the minds and hearts of everyone on your sales team. It takes *personal* leadership and *demonstrated*, ongoing commitment on the part of the Sales professional (YOU) to show, employees and customers alike, the *'true essence'* of Customer Service.

Sales isn't part of the game; it is the game!

As a true sales professional, "Customer Service is not just *'a part'* of your business – Customer service *'is'* your business!"

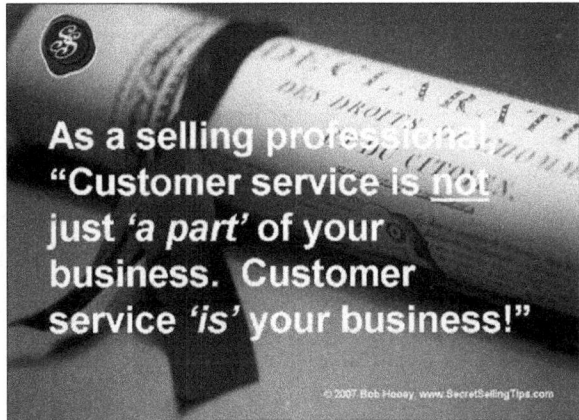

As a selling professional "Customer service is **not** just *'a part'* of your business. Customer service *'is'* your business!"

© 2007 Bob Hooey, www.SecretSellingTips.com

This small change in focus can result in a substantial change in productivity and profitability. A small change in focus and action can result in a substantial change in customer referrals and repeat business.

Point to Ponder: *"Above all, we wish to avoid having a dissatisfied customer. We consider our customers a part of our organization, and we want them to feel free to make any criticism they see fit in regard to our merchandise or service. Sell practical, tested merchandise at reasonable profit, treat your customers like human beings – and they will always come back."* L.L. Bean

Here are our 7 'Be-Attitudes.' We hope they will be of assistance in sharing the importance of customer service as an integral part of the sales process all year.

1. **Be professional** – putting the customer first. Presenting yourself or your company in a professional manner. A sales professional is always looking for ways to help the customer and to make their life better by offering products or services that work.

2. **Be polite** – wouldn't you expect to be given consideration and respect? Remember to give your clients/customers the same courtesy, regardless of the kind of day you may be having.

3. **Be prompt** – do your best to not keep customers waiting. If you promise something, do everything you can to deliver on time, or call and let the customer know exactly what time to expect you. Try not to keep a customer waiting on the phone or in your store either.

4. **Be proud** – you are an expert, a solutions provider to your clients/customers. Be proud of your expertise and ability to help them make wise choices.

5. **Be personal** – remember your customers are individuals. Don't you hate it when people treat you like just another number? Make a commitment to treat every customer as an individual – it will make him or her feel special. Sales professionals know and prove 'They are special!'

6. **Be persistent** – good service isn't *always* given on the first encounter. Being persistent in your efforts to serve and solve their problems. If your client/customer has a problem with your service or product, persistence in making sure they are satisfied, or problem is rectified to their needs is essential. This is where you prove your claim to being a sales professional.

7. **Be patient** – some customers need a little more time or assistance to make their selection. Taking the time, especially with our seniors or children is the true sign of a sales professional.

These *7 'Be-Attitudes'* of customer service may not guarantee you success in your sales career or business. Lack of their application can seriously harm it. They do, when applied, give you one of the foundations for success in building a sales career or business that will still be here in the future to serve your customers actively and profitably.

Challenge: Invest a few minutes in honest reflection on your application of these 7 Be-Attitudes.

- How did you do?
- Did you find some that were strengths for you?
- Did you find some that needed improvement?
- What are you committed to changing to bring them to your role as a sales professional?

Note from Bob: We hope you have enjoyed your journey with us and that it has been a profitable one in both your growth and your profitability in your role as a sales professional. All the best in your sales career.

We look forward to sharing ideas and additional volumes with you for many years to come. For other books by Bob, visit www.successpublications.ca

Drop me a note and share some of your success stories. bhooey@mcsnet.ca

PRO-tip: Sales secrets to help guide you

Don't celebrate closing a sale; celebrate opening a relationship if you want to build a long-term successful enterprise. It is not your client and prospect's job to remember you. It is your responsibility to make sure they do not have the chance to forget you. The real sale comes after the sale, reselling the customer – you have to retain their business.

© **Patricia Fripp,** www.Fripp.com

Copyright and License Notes

Sales Success Secrets
Idea-rich secret selling tips — Volume One

Bob 'Idea Man' Hooey, Accredited Speaker, 2011 Spirit of CAPS recipient. *Prolific author of 30 plus business, leadership, and career success publications*

Photos of Bob: **Dov Friedman**, www.photographybyDov.com
Bonnie-Jean McAllister, www.elantraphotography.com
Editorial, layout and design: **Irene Gaudet**, Vitrak Creative Services (a division of Creativity Corner Inc.), www.vitrakcreative.com

ISBN: 978-1-896737-89-8

Printed in the United States 10 9 8 7 6 5 4 3 2 1
www.SuccessPublications.ca — a division of Creativity Corner Inc.
Box 10, Egremont, AB T0A 0Z0
www.successpublications.ca
Creative office: +1-780-736-0009 (MST)

Acknowledgements, Credits, and Disclaimers

תודה
Dankie Gracias
Спасибо شكرا
Merci Takk
Köszönjük Terima kasih
Grazie Dziękujemy Dėkojame
Ďakujeme Vielen Dank Paldies
Kiitos Täname teid 謝謝
Thank You Tak
感謝您 Obrigado Teşekkür Ederiz
Σας Ευχαριστούμ 감사합니다
ขอบคุณ
Bedankt Děkujeme vám
ありがとうございます
Tack

As with each of my books, a very special dedication of this piece of myself, to the two people who meant the most to me, my folks **Ron and Marge Hooey.** Sadly, both my parents left this earthly realm in 1999.

To my inspiring wife, professional proof-reader and publications coach, **Irene Gaudet**, who loves, encourages, and supports me in my quest to continue sharing my **Ideas At Work!** across the world. Thank you seems so inadequate for your timely work in helping make my writing and my client service better! I love the time we spend together!

My thanks to the many people who have encouraged me in my growth as a leader, speaker, salesman, and engaging trainer in each area of expertise. To Peter Chapman, Joanne Blake, Terry Pithers, Barbara Glanz, Joe Bonura, Patricia Fripp, Tim Breithaupt, Jill Konrath, for kindly allowing us to share your wisdom.

To my colleagues and friends in the National Speakers Association (NSA), the Canadian Association of Professional Speakers (CAPS), and the Global Speakers Federation (GSF) who continually challenge me to strive for success and increased excellence.

To my great audiences, leaders, students, coaching clients, and readers across the globe who share their experiences and enjoyment of my work. Your positive and supportive feedback encourages me to keep working on additional programs and success publications like this updated version. My experience with you creates the foundation for additional real-life experiences I can take from the stage to the page, the classroom to the boardroom.

My thanks to a select few friends for your ongoing support and 'constructive' abuse. You know who you are. ☺

Disclaimer

We have not attempted to cite all the authorities and sources consulted in the preparation of this book. To do so would require much more space than is available. The list would include departments of various governments, libraries, industrial institutions, periodicals, and many individuals. Inspiration was drawn from many sources, including other books by the author; in this adapted creation of **'Secret Sales Success.'**

This book is written and designed to provide information on more effective use of your time, as a life and leadership enhancement guide. It is sold with the 'explicit' understanding that the publisher and/or the author are not engaged in rendering legal, accounting, or other professional services. If legal or other expert assistance is required, the services of a competent professional in your geographic area should be sought.

It is not the purpose of this book to reprint all the information that is otherwise available. Its primary purpose is to complement, amplify, and supplement other books and reference materials already available. You are encouraged to search out and study all the available material, learn as much as possible, and tailor the information to your individual needs. This will help to enhance your success in being a more effective businessman, sales- person, leader or professional by applying active listening skills.

Every effort has been made to make this book as complete and as accurate as possible within the scope of its focus. However, there may be mistakes, both typographical and in content or attribution. Graphics are royalty free or under license. Care has been taken to trace ownership of copyright material contained in this volume. The publisher will gladly receive information that will allow him to rectify any reference or credit line in subsequent editions. This book should be used only as a general guide and not as the ultimate source of information. Furthermore, this book contains information that is current only up to the date of publication.

The purpose of Sales Success Secrets – Volume One *is to educate and entertain; perhaps to inform and to inspire. It is certainly to challenge its readers to learn and apply its secrets and tips, to challenge them to enhance their skills and leverage their time to create more productive outcomes. The author and publisher shall have neither liability nor responsibility to any person or entity with respect to any loss or damage caused, or alleged to have been caused, directly or indirectly, by the information contained in this book.*

Bob's Publications

Bob is a prolific author who has been capturing and sharing his wisdom and experience in printed and electronic forms for the past twenty-five plus years.

In addition to the following publications, he has written for consumer, corporate, professional associations, trade, and on-line publications. He has also been engaged to write and assist on publications by other writers and companies. He loves seeing his Ideas At Work!

Leadership, business, and career development series

Running TOO Fast (8th edition 2022)
Legacy of Leadership (3rd edition 2022)
Make ME Feel Special! (6th edition 2022)
Why Didn't I 'THINK' of That? (6th edition 2022)
Speaking for Success! (9th edition 2022)
THINK Beyond the First Sale (3rd edition 2022)
Prepare Yourself to Win! (3rd edition 2017)
The early years… 1998-2009 – A Tip of the Hat collection (2020)
The saga continues… 2010-2019 - A Tip of the Hat collection (2020)
Sales Success Secrets – Idea-rich Secret Selling Tips, Volume One (2022)
Sales Success Secrets – Idea-rich Secret Selling Tips, Volume Two (2022)

Bob's Mini-book success series

The Courage to Lead! (4th edition 2017)
Creative Conflict (3rd edition 2017)
THINK Before You Ink! (3rd edition 2017)
Running to Win! (2nd edition 2017)
How to Generate More Sales (4th edition 2017)
Unleash your Business Potential (3rd edition 2017)
Maximize Meetings (2019)
Learn to Listen (4th edition 2020)
Creativity Counts! (2nd edition 2016)

Create Your Future! (3rd edition 2017)
Get to Yes! *Idea-rich introductions to subtle art of creative persuasion in sales and negotiation* (2020)

Bob's Pocket Wisdom series

Pocket Wisdom for Speakers (updated 2019)
Pocket Wisdom for Leaders – Power of One! (updated 2019)
Pocket Wisdom for Innovators (updated 2020)
Pocket Wisdom for Business Builders – My 'Next' Million Dollar Idea (updated 2020)
Pocket Wisdom for Sales Professionals – Secret Sales Tips (updated 2020)

Quick reads (2017-2021) - more to come

LEAD! *Idea-rich leadership success strategies*
CREATE! *Idea-rich strategies for enhanced innovation*
TIME! *Idea-rich tips for enhanced performance and productivity*
SERVE! *Idea-rich strategies for enhanced customer service*
SPEAK! *Idea-rich tips and techniques for great presentations*
CREATIVE CONFLICT *Idea-rich leadership for team success*
SELL *Idea-rich techniques for sales success*
SUCCEED! *Idea-rich strategies to succeed in business, despite global disruptions (2020)*
WRITE ON! *Idea-rich tips and techniques to bring your book into pixels or print*
My Story Journal *Idea-rich tips to enhance your writing and speaking success using stories (2020)*

Co-authored books created by Bob

Quantum Success – 3 volume series (2006)
In the Company of Leaders (95th anniversary Edition 2019)
Foundational Success (2nd Edition 2013)
PIVOT To Present: *Idea-rich strategies to deliver your virtual message with impact (2020)*

Visit: www.SuccessPublications.ca for more information

Visit: **www.PandemicPublishers.com** for a selection of journals, notebooks, and sketchbooks **New for 2021.**

What They Say About Bob 'Idea Man' Hooey

As I travel across North America, and more recently around the globe, presenting live and on-line, sharing my **Ideas At Work!**, I am fortunate to get feedback and comments from my audiences and colleagues who give me a listen. I so appreciate my audiences and clients for this privilege.

These comments come from people who have been touched, challenged, or simply enjoyed themselves in one of my live or virtual sessions. I hope to add you to that list.

I'd love to come and share some ideas with your organization and teams, either live or on-line. Visit: www.ideaman.net or www.BobHooey.training for more information

'I've known Bob for several years and follow his activities in business with interest. I originally met Bob when he spoke for a Rotary Leadership Institute and got to know him better when he came to Vladivostok, Russia to speak to our leadership. When you spoke, I thought you were one of us because you talked about our challenges just like yours. You could understand the others, which makes you a great speaker!'
Andrey Konyushok, Rotary International District 2225 Governor 2012-2013, far eastern Russia

'We greatly appreciate the energy and effort you put into researching and adapting your keynote to make it more meaningful to our member councils.
Early feedback from our delegates indicates that this year's convention was one of our most successful events yet, and we thank you for your contribution to this success.'
Larry Goodhope, Executive Director Alberta Association of Municipal Districts and Counties

'Bob is one of those rare individuals who knows how to tackle obstacles in life to reach his dreams. He takes each as a learning experience and stretches for more. His compassion and genuine interest in others make him an exceptional coach.'
Cindy Kindret, Training Manager, Silk FM Radio

'I still get comments from people about your presentation. Only a few speakers have left an impression that lasts that long. You hit a spot with the tourism people.'

Janet Bell, Yukon Economic Forums

'Thank you, Bob; it is always a pleasure to see a true professional at work. You have made the name 'Speaker' stand out as a truism - someone who encourages people to examine their lives and make adjustments. The personal stories you shared with your audience made such a great impression on everyone. The comments indicated you hit people right where it is important - in their hearts. Each of those in your audience took away a new feeling of personal success and encouragement.'
Sherry Knight, Dimension Eleven Human Resources and Communications

'Without doubt, I have gained immeasurable self-assurance. Bob, your patience and your encouragement has been much appreciated. I strongly recommend your course to anyone looking for self-improvement and professional development.'
Jeannie Mura, Human Resources Chevron Canada

'I am pleased to recommend Bob 'Idea Man' Hooey to any organization looking for a charismatic, confident speaker and seminar leader. I have seen Bob in action on several occasions, and he is ALWAYS on! Bob has the ability to grab his audience's attention and keep it. Quite simply, if Bob is involved - your program or seminar is guaranteed to succeed.'
Maurice Laving, Coordinator Training and Development, London Drugs

'I have found Bob's attention to detail and his ability to fine tune his seminars to match the time frame and needs of the audience to be a valuable asset to our educational Program.'
Patsy Schell, Executive Director Surrey Chamber of Commerce

'What a great conference. It was a great pleasure meeting with you at the Ritz Carlton, Cancun and I shall look forward to hopefully welcoming you and your family in Dublin, Ireland someday.' **A. Paul Ryan**, Petronva Corporation, Dublin, Ireland

'Congratulations on the Spirit of CAPS Award. You have worked long and hard on behalf of CAPS ...helped many speakers including me and richly deserve this award. Well done my friend.' **Peter Legge**, CSP, Hof, CPAE

'I had the pleasure of hearing and watching Bob Hooey deliver a keynote speech several years ago when he gave a presentation at a Toastmasters International Convention. Bob impressed me greatly with his professionalism, energy, and ability to connect with his audience while giving them value.' Dr. **Dilip Abayasekara**, DTM, Accredited Speaker, Past Toastmasters International President

Engage Bob For Your Sales Teams

'I have been so excited working with Bob Hooey, as he has given inspiration and motivation to our leadership team members. Both at the Brick Warehouse – Alberta and at Art Van Furniture – Michigan; with his years of experience in working with business executives and his humorous and delightful packaging of his material, he makes learning with Bob a real joy. But most importantly, anyone who encounters his material is the better for it.'
Kim Yost, CEO Art Van Furniture *(retired)*, former CEO The Brick

- Motivate your teams, your employees, and your leaders to 'productively' grow and 'profitably' succeed!
- Protect your conference investment - leverage your training dollars.
- Enhance your professional career and sell more products and services.
- Equip and motivate your leaders and their teams to grow and succeed, 'even' in tough times!
- Leverage your time to enhance your skills, equip your teams, and better serve your clients.
- Leverage your leadership and investment of time to leave a significant legacy!
- **Engage him to deliver his sales and management programs virtually anywhere in the world.**

Call today to engage sales-author, award winning, inspirational leadership keynote speaker, leaders' success coach, and employee development trainer, **Bob 'Idea Man' Hooey** and his innovative, audience based, results-focused, **Ideas At Work!** for your next company, convention, leadership, staff, training, or association event. You'll be glad you did!

Call +1-780-736-0009 to connect with **Bob 'Idea Man' Hooey**
Bob's personal email: bhooey@mcsnet.ca

The Most Important 'Creative' Questions in the Sales Process

Ask yourself: Why would this prospect (client) be interested in buying my products or services? Or, dealing with me?

Ask yourself: Have I done my homework?

Ask the Client: What is the most critical issue or concern you'd like to resolve about _____?

Follow up: What makes you say that? What else causes you concern?

Ask the Client: Are you ready to get started? May we have your business?

Ask the Client: Who else do you know that would have a need for my products or services? May I use your name? (Secret to generating more sales through the power of referrals.)

Ask the Client: How have we been doing? Are there any adjustments we need to make to better serve you and provide for your needs? (Secret of effective customer service.)

The sales process is all about creativity: Creating profitable opportunities to better serve your clients. If you don't investigate their needs and desires, how will you find out where you can be of benefit to them?

Asking for help and involving them in the process will build your career.

The foundation for creativity (in sales) is built by asking probing questions and then using those answers in working in partnership with your clients to create the solution they need.

Excerpted from **'Generating more Sales'** *by Bob 'Idea Man' Hooey*

www.ingramcontent.com/pod-product-compliance
Lightning Source LLC
Chambersburg PA
CBHW071708210326
41597CB00017B/2392